SPEAKING IN TONGUES
Silencing The Debate

Written by
Dr. Anthony Revis

authorHOUSE™

Milton Keynes, UK

AuthorHouse™
1663 Liberty Drive, Suite 200
Bloomington, IN 47403
www.authorhouse.com
Phone: 1-800-839-8640

AuthorHouse™ UK Ltd.
500 Avebury Boulevard
Central Milton Keynes, MK9 2BE
www.authorhouse.co.uk
Phone: 08001974150

Speaking in Tongues – Silencing the Debate

First published by AuthorHouse 4/11/2006

ISBN: 1-4259-2052-7 (sc)

Printed in the United States of America
Bloomington, Indiana

This book is printed on acid-free paper.

All scripture quotes are either from the Holy Bible, King James Version; Holy Bible, New International Version, Copyright © 1873, 1978, 1984 by International Bible Society, Colorado Springs, Colorado; or Holy Bible, Amplified Version, Copyright © 1954, 1958, 1962, 1964, 1965, 1987, the Lockman Foundation, LaHabra, California. Used by permission.

Anthony Revis Ministries
11225 Sarle Road
Freeland, Michigan 48623

PREFACE

There are some very important insights about speaking in tongues and its relationship to prophecy and salvation that will open your eyes to greater revelations about who God is in your life. I invite you to find out what they are.

Prior to writing this book, had you asked me whether it seemed useful to write yet another book on the subject of speaking in tongues, I might have said no. After all, this subject has been well written about and discussed almost exhaustively by Christians and non-Christians alike for centuries. But here I am writing a book on the subject of speaking in tongues, nonetheless.

I realize I am walking into what tends to be a controversial area. But there are some very important insights about speaking in tongues and its relationship to prophecy and salvation that will open your eyes to greater revelations about who God is in your life. I invite you to find out what they are.

This book does not attempt to explicitly prove the existence of the gift of tongues. Neither does it try to convince you that you should speak in tongues. What this book does, however, is set in order key biblical perspectives on the topic of speaking in tongues.

This book particularly discusses how the gift of speaking in tongues relates to prophecy and salvation. It does so by focusing primarily on 1 Corinthians 14 and offering my commentary on this and other relevant scripture passages.

I do not bother you with Greek, Latin, Hebrew or other scholarly terms and definitions in this book. I do not discuss issues of syntax and linguistics at all. I keep it simple. I only use the Bible and simple annotations to help unveil the truth about speaking in tongues.

Psalm 49 ³My mouth will speak words of wisdom; the utterance from my heart will give understanding.

I hope this book blesses you as you read it as much as it blessed me while writing it for you. I hope it brings a fresh perspective to your views on the gift of speaking in tongues. And I hope it silences the debate on speaking in tongues for you, once and for all.

Chapter 1. Why the Debate

I am convinced that a careful reading of 1 Corinthians 14 will easily settle many of the issues surrounding the gift called speaking in tongues.

The topic of speaking in tongues has been a troublesome subject for some Christians. Some within the church have debated its validity and appropriateness ever since the first recorded event on the Day of Pentecost in Acts 2. This was almost two thousand years ago. Discussions become even more challenging when one considers the relationship between prophetic preaching of the gospel and speaking in tongues.

The Apostle Paul set out to clarify the relationship between the gift of prophecy and speaking in tongues in his first letter to the Corinthian church. It is recorded in 1 Corinthians 14. Although this passage does speak clearly for itself on the matter of both prophecy and speaking in tongues, it is often misrepresented.

There certainly appears to be a problem for many Christians who stand firmly along strong denominational lines and preferences with regard to speaking in tongues. Many stand without the benefit of having at least done a self-study of the Bible on the topic. Some are satisfied with conclusions of religious tradition more so than spiritual insight. This causes problems. Paul also speaks clearly on this matter as well.

Colossians 2 ⁸See to it that no one takes you captive through hollow and deceptive philosophy, which depends on human tradition and the basic principles of this world rather than on Christ.

These preferences and positions of "deceptive philosophy" lead to weaknesses in the interpretation of scripture. This then leads to weaknesses in Christian living. This ultimately robs Christians of opportunities to experience the fullness of what God has and how He wants them to live. These religiously motivated preferences also enslave the minds of those who might otherwise see the light of the gospel.

2 Corinthians 4 ³And even if our gospel is veiled, it is veiled to those who are perishing. ⁴The god of this age has blinded the minds of unbelievers, so that they cannot see the light of the gospel of the glory of Christ, who is the image of God.

There clearly are biases within many Christian circles with respect to the subject of spiritual gifts. These biases seem to exist even more so with regard to speaking in tongues.

I am not suggesting it is the purposeful intent of anyone within the body of Christ to mislead people on this topic. I do not believe any anointed man or woman of God wants to enslave themselves or others to specific religious philosophies or denominational edicts. We are called to live beyond such constraints.

Galatians 5 ¹Stand fast therefore in the liberty wherewith Christ hath made us free, and be not entangled again with the yoke of bondage.

Unfortunately, many have drawn very strong battle lines on the issue of speaking in tongues, and they refuse to move. Some are consumed with either proving or disproving points of theology. They have neglected to simply let the word of God speak for itself.

2 Timothy 2 ¹⁵Do your best to present yourself to God as one approved, a workman who does not need to be ashamed and who correctly handles the word of truth.

Some do find it more difficult than others to grasp the more perplexing concepts about spiritual gifts. It is not always easy to convey such ideas in simple terms. The concept of speaking in tongues is especially difficult; where you might make utterances that you don't fully understand. We just do not have the spirit-minded capacity to completely understand such works of God on our own. But if we trust Him, He will supply us with sufficient faith-filled understanding to act in His will.

Colossians 1 ⁹So we have continued praying for you ever since we first heard about you. We ask God to give you a complete understanding of what he wants to do in your lives, and we ask him to make you wise with spiritual wisdom.

The Bible contains many events and occurrences that do not make sense outside of the realm of faith. However, as believers, we have come to know that these events are very real. Faith allows us to see them and experience the tangible evidence of their impact. By faith, we know God sends spiritual gifts beyond our complete, mental comprehension. He certainly sends gifts outside of our personal comfort zones. So it is not possible to comprehend all the works of God. They are too vast even for the greatest minds among us!

Ecclesiastes 8 ¹⁶When I applied my mind to know wisdom and to observe man's labor on earth—his eyes not seeing sleep day or night— ¹⁷then I saw all that God has done. No one can comprehend what goes on under the sun. Despite all his efforts to search it out, man cannot discover its meaning. Even if a wise man claims he knows, he cannot really comprehend it.

That is why we need faith. Faith takes us to levels that we would not otherwise reach. Faith works outside of us to bless us. It is likewise true for spiritual gifts. They work beyond our current situation to bring us into a new level of spiritual reality with God. And God's gifts are sometimes unbelievable!

Psalm 145 ⁵They will speak of the glorious splendor of your majesty, and I will meditate on your wonderful works.

Spiritual gifts require a leap of faith. Faith makes spiritual gifts come alive. You then see what faith produces!

Hebrews 11 ¹Now faith is the substance of things hoped for, the evidence of things not seen.

So I am asking you to take a faith walk with me as you read the remainder of this book. I am asking you to reexamine the biblical subject of speaking in tongues, particularly as it relates to prophecy. If you are weak in faith, prayer can help.

Luke 17 ⁵The apostles said to the Lord, "Increase our faith!"

This will be a faith walk through 1 Corinthians 14. In this passage, Paul attempts to lift the veil and break the shackles from the church on the topic of speaking in tongues and its relationship to prophecy. Unfortunately, it seems to have created more controversy than certainly Paul envisioned it would. However, a careful read of 1 Corinthians 14 will easily settle many of the issues surrounding this gift called speaking in tongues. It will become apparent what Paul's original intent was with regard to speaking in tongues as it relates to prophecy. You will see why and how Paul set these gifts so clearly in order for the church.

1 Corinthians 14 ⁴⁰But everything should be done in a fitting and orderly way.

I will show Paul's original intent by first examining the purpose and power of prophecy. I will then show the clear Bible connection between prophecy and speaking in tongues. Afterwards, I will show the relationship between speaking in tongues, prophecy and salvation. As a consequence, a more rewarding biblical perspective will result that shows God's anointed purpose in prophecy and in speaking in tongues.

So let us look at the topics of both prophecy and speaking in tongues with somewhat more focus on speaking in tongues. Let us discover God's answers to at least the following questions:

1. Is there a gift called speaking in tongues?

2. Did Paul say speaking in tongues should be abolished?

3. How does speaking in tongues relate to prophecy and salvation?

4. When does speaking in tongues happen?

5. What does speaking in tongues do?

6. Why are there utterances?

Chapter 2. Spiritual Gifts for the Church

Nowhere in 1 Corinthian 14 does Paul ever say speaking in tongues had ended or should be permanently stopped. Neither does Paul say the people who were speaking in tongues were excited babblers.

I maintain the position that every word in the Bible is spoken truth from God, even when I cannot comprehend it all. That is my basic premise when reading the Bible. I choose to believe all of God's word even when I do not understand it all or understand its relevance. I accept the fact that God is bigger and wiser than me.

> *Isaiah 55* [8]*"For my thoughts are not your thoughts, neither are your ways my ways," declares the LORD.*

You must accept the fact that God can perform wonders within the church that might transcend your level of understanding and faith. He can also work through methods that are not completely comfortable to you. God's truth is not validated by your comfort. It is validated by His word.

> *Proverbs 30* [5]*Every word of God is flawless; he is a shield to those who take refuge in him.* [6]*Do not add to his words, or he will rebuke you and prove you a liar.*

Therefore, let us see what God's word has to say about spiritual gifts, particularly prophecy and speaking in tongues. Do these spiritual gifts exist? What was Paul's position on them?

An unbiased reading of only a portion of 1 Corinthians 14 is a good place to start.

> *1 Corinthians 14* [1]*Follow the way of love and eagerly desire spiritual gifts, especially the gift of prophecy.* [2]*For anyone who speaks in a tongue does not speak to men but to God. Indeed, no one understands him; he utters mysteries with his spirit.* [3]*But everyone who prophesies speaks to men for their strengthening, encouragement and comfort.* [4]*He who speaks in a tongue edifies himself, but he who prophesies edifies the church.* [5]*I would like every one of you to speak in tongues, but I would rather have you prophesy. He who prophesies is greater than one who speaks in tongues, unless he interprets, so that the church may be edified.*

The above verses clearly establish that there were spiritual gifts in the church at Corinth. Two of the gifts were prophecy and speaking in tongues. The Corinthian church did not deny the fact of their existence.

Unfortunately, these two gifts had caused conflict among the Corinthian believers. This was the reason Paul wrote the letter to them. It was intended to settle the confusion that had erupted over these two spiritual gifts, especially with regard to the place and purpose of speaking in tongues.

Spiritual gifts are still causing some conflict and discomfort within the church today. For many, this conflict has led to a complete disregard and denial of the existence of gifts altogether. This tends to be especially true for speaking in tongues. But the Apostle Paul in 1 Corinthians 14 affirms that both prophecy and speaking in tongues are gifts for the church.

Therefore, whether you speak in tongues or not is irrelevant to its existence. Speaking in tongues exist. God's word establishes this fact. Nowhere in 1 Corinthian 14 does Paul ever say speaking in tongues does not exist, has ended or should be permanently stopped. Neither does Paul say the people who were speaking in tongues were excited babblers.

So it seems fruitless to debate the existence of the gift of tongues. It exists.

Not only do we learn speaking in tongues exists, but we also learn that it is all right to want this spiritual gift. Paul said to "eagerly desire spiritual gifts," which means to be excited about gifts!

It is great that we can be excited, not fearful, about the spiritual gifts God has for us. Therefore, there is absolutely no reason not to want speaking in tongues and prophecy as gifts.

Also, these two gifts are not at odds with other gifts in the church. They support them. For example, God calls people into specific ministry roles and positions. The Bible is very clear in showing that these are gifts, too. God places anointed men and women in the church according to His divine purpose. These gifts work together with other gifts to benefit the church.

> *Ephesians 4 [11]It was he who gave some to be apostles, some to be prophets, some to be evangelists, and some to be pastors and teachers, [12]to prepare God's people for works of service, so that the body of Christ may be built up.*

The Ephesians 4 gifts are the specific offices to which God places leadership or "headship" within the church. These pastoral or overseer gifts are divine callings to headship administration. However, they do not dismiss God's sovereign right to deposit other specific spiritual gifts within the general body of the church for "sonship" or discipleship assignments. In other words, God's non-pastoral gifts are for the purpose of sonship and service operations. They promote opportunities for all believers to operate according to the Holy Spirit in the ministry of the church and their individual lives.

> *1 Corinthians 7 [17]Nevertheless, each one should retain the place in life that the Lord assigned to him and to which God has called him. This is the rule I lay down in all the churches.*

The gifts of prophecy and speaking in tongues are sources of strength in executing God's plan. So it is wonderful to know you can eagerly seek gifts for your assigned place within the body of Christ.

Let me restate what Paul wrote to the church.

> *1 Corinthians 14 [1]...eagerly desire spiritual gifts...*

Spiritual gifts are available to you. You can desire them. There is no command against wanting spiritual gifts. And if you sincerely seek them with an inspired sense and awareness of who God is, He will grant them to you.

> _Psalm 37_ [4]_Delight yourself in the LORD and he will give you the desires of your heart._

Chapter 3. Priority of Prophecy and Tongues

When Paul placed the priority on prophecy, he did not make speaking in tongues an inferior gift. He simply set the church in order.

In 1 Corinthians 14, Paul discusses both speaking in tongues and prophecy. These are spiritual gifts to the church. Some read 1 Corinthians 14 to suggest that Paul is in favor of prophecy but against speaking in tongues. But is he?

Let us now read again Paul's letter to discover his original intent for these two spiritual gifts. Let us find out in particular whether he was putting prophecy at odds with speaking in tongues.

> *1 Corinthians 14 ¹Follow the way of love and eagerly desire spiritual gifts, especially the gift of prophecy. ²For anyone who speaks in a tongue does not speak to men but to God. Indeed, no one understands him; he utters mysteries with his spirit. ³But everyone who prophesies speaks to men for their strengthening, encouragement and comfort. ⁴He who speaks in a tongue edifies himself, but he who prophesies edifies the church. ⁵I would like every one of you to speak in tongues, but I would rather have you prophesy. He who prophesies is greater than one who speaks in tongues, unless he interprets, so that the church may be edified.*

As you read 1 Corinthians 14, you discover there is a priority assigned to the gifts within the church. Paul teaches there should be a priority placed on the gift of prophecy. In other words, if you were forced to choose one gift, then prophecy should be chosen. This is a very important point, the reason for which will become even more evident in the next chapters. For now, we note there is a clear priority placed on prophecy.

> *1 Corinthians 14 ¹Follow the way of love and eagerly desire spiritual gifts, especially the gift of prophecy.*

Paul said you should especially desire prophecy. But he did not say you could not have other gifts, too. He did not say you could not have speaking in tongues as well.

However, there is a clear priority placed on prophecy. This point cannot be denied. Paul even restates his position again in 1 Corinthians 14:5. He puts emphasis on prophecy.

1 Corinthians 14 ⁵I would like every one of you to speak in tongues, but I would rather have you prophesy. He who prophesies is greater than one who speaks in tongues, unless he interprets, so that the church may be edified.

Paul said, "I would rather have you prophesy." So there is a priority for these gifts. Prophecy is prioritized ahead of speaking in tongues when a choice must be made. But priority does not mean superiority.

When Paul placed the priority on prophecy, he did not make speaking in tongues an inferior gift. He simply set the church in order.

There are similar biblical references to placing priority on gifts, without meaning superiority. Reading 1 Corinthians 13:13 is insightful in this regard.

1 Corinthians 13 ¹³And now these three remain: faith, hope and love. But the greatest [priority] of these is love. [Revis annotation]

1 Corinthians 13:13 places priority on love. But this does not cancel out the value of faith and hope. No one in the body of Christ would ever argue that faith is not critical to the church. The scripture clearly lets us know faith is critical.

Hebrews 11 ⁶And without faith it is impossible to please God, because anyone who comes to him must believe that he exists and that he rewards those who earnestly seek him.

Neither would any believer speak against the precious power of hope. Hope is essential to faith.

Romans 8 ²⁴For in this hope we were saved. But hope that is seen is no hope at all. Who hopes for what he already has?

It would be unheard of for a believer to ever speak against the value of faith or hope. Believers clearly recognize the importance of faith and hope. And they have no problem at all with the special emphasis and priority placed on love.

The gifts of prophecy and speaking in tongues are likewise related. Prophecy has priority with regard to the church's public spiritual events. But its priority does not lessen the value and importance of speaking in tongues.

Priority does not require superiority. Spiritual gifts can work quite well in their respective places without negating each other's value. Therefore, the gift of prophecy can have the priority position without canceling the gift of speaking in tongues.

Chapter 4. From Prophecy to Tangible Outcomes

Only God can transform mere words and utterances into mental concepts and spiritual revelations that move people to act by faith. He can even deposit tangible objects in their lives where needed.

There are certain fundamental principles about how God works that are important to understanding His gifts. One of those principles involves the position from which God starts His works with man, or how "things" come into being. The principle is very simply this:

Everything from God starts in the spirit realm as its point of origin, including those things we see, touch, smell and hear, or otherwise experience as physical events.

Events of God's choosing start in the spirit realm or spirit-mind of God and are afterwards manifested in the physical dimension of man. It is this move or action of the spirit that leads to tangibly, deliverable outcomes. In other words, what we receive from God starts in heaven by His spirit and is transformed into an outcome we could use. It often shows up in a tangible form.

We see the first evidence of this principle of spiritual concepts leading to tangible outcomes in Genesis 1.

Genesis 1 ¹In the beginning God created the heavens and the earth. ²Now the earth was formless and empty, darkness was over the surface of the deep, and the Spirit of God was hovering over the waters. ³And God said, "Let there be light," and there was light.

So a move of the spirit of God produces a physical outcome in a form man can interact with.

God's actions start this way because the spirit of God is the very nature of God. And God does not go against His own nature. It is impossible for Him to do so. Therefore, all interactions with Him must somehow conform to a spiritual nature or a spiritual law. This principle helps clarify the importance of seeking a spiritual relationship with God.

John 4 ²⁴God is spirit, and his worshipers [intimate people] must worship in spirit and in truth." [Revis annotation]

God uses His nature, His very spirit, to bring about His will. It is by God's spirit that we come to know we are saved children of God.

Romans 8 ¹⁶The Spirit himself testifies with our spirit that we are God's children.

One of the works of prophecy is activation or awakening of your spirit. Your activated spirit is caused by a move of God. Prophecy gets you ready for a refreshing, tangible manifestation in your life.

Something miraculous happens because of prophecy. It brings life to your spirit where there is none and improves life where it already exists. It brings you from darkened times into God's perfect light.

1 Peter 2 ⁹But ye are a chosen generation, a royal priesthood, an holy nation, a peculiar people; that ye should shew forth the praises of him who hath called [prophesied] you out of darkness into his marvellous light [life]. [Revis annotation]

God's spirit-based works are amazing. We see them through actions resulting from His spoken and written prophecies. Only God can transform mere words and utterances into mental concepts and spiritual revelations that move people to act by faith. He can even deposit tangible objects in their lives where needed, based on prophecy. These tangible forms are what we call blessings. Some are so amazing that we call them miracles!

Job 5 ⁹He [God] performs wonders that cannot be fathomed, miracles that cannot be counted. [Revis annotation]

Psalm 77 ¹⁴You are the God who performs miracles; you display your power among the peoples.

So prophecy starts in the spirit realm and shows up in the tangible or physical environment. That is how you know it is God at work or it is a move of God.

That is what happened on the Day of Pentecost. God moved in the spirit and it showed up in the physical experience as a miracle!

> *Acts 2 ¹When the day of Pentecost came, they were all together in one place. ²Suddenly a sound like the blowing of a violent wind came from heaven and filled the whole house where they were sitting. ³They saw what seemed to be tongues of fire that separated and came to rest on each of them. ⁴All of them were filled with the Holy Spirit and began to speak in other tongues as the Spirit enabled them.*

The Day of Pentecost was not a spontaneous event, although it did show up suddenly to the disciples. It was not the result of sheer excitement or exuberance, although those involved were excited. Instead, it was the result of a pre-ordained, spirit-filled prophecy. The most recent prophecy to these disciples was recorded in Acts 1:8.

> *Acts 1 ⁸But you will receive power when the Holy Spirit comes on you; and you will be my witnesses in Jerusalem, and in all Judea and Samaria, and to the ends of the earth."*

The Acts 1:8 prophecy activated the spirit of those in the house. It yielded the tangible outcome of utterances from the mouth of the people. This outcome was a new experience from the spirit of God. God moved to create an event that man had never experienced before. The new event was called speaking in tongues. It initiated the earth-based gift of tongues. This event could not be described by any clear process of man because it was outside of man's previous experiences. It was beyond man's expectations. It was an awesome new miracle at work.

Speaking in tongues was a new spiritual transfer from heaven into the spiritual ranks of man on the Day of

Pentecost. Jesus had prophesied a unique day of baptism by the Holy Spirit was coming. And it did with great power!

Acts 1 ⁴On one occasion, while he was eating with them, he gave them this command: "Do not leave Jerusalem, but wait for the gift my Father promised, which you have heard me speak about. ⁵For John baptized with water, but in a few days you will be baptized with the Holy Spirit."

It is exciting to notice the similarity between what Jesus said in Acts 1:4 and what Paul said in 1 Corinthians 14:1.

1 Corinthians 14 ¹Follow the way of love and eagerly desire spiritual gifts, especially the gift of prophecy.

Jesus said in Acts 1:4, "do not leave Jerusalem, but wait for the gift." Paul said in 1 Corinthians 14:1 to "eagerly desire spiritual gifts." Both these phrases suggest a sense of strong expectation of something wonderful and special to occur. And it certainly did.

Clearly, no born-again believer would ever deny that the gifting of the Holy Spirit is a wonderful experience! The specific outpouring of the Holy Spirit on the Day of Pentecost and for much of the church thereafter was evidenced by speaking in tongues. And it seems clear that Paul was not saying the church should never speak in tongues when he wrote 1 Corinthians 14. Therefore, there is no good reason for the church today to expect any less of God's gifting. Speaking in tongues is the outcome of the specific baptism of the Holy Spirit.

Unfortunately, for many today, speaking in tongues is an event still outside of their experiences. It is still foreign to many who are genuine members of the body of Christ. But it does not have to be so. The gift is available to all believers who eagerly seek it.

So on the Day of Pentecost, the prophecy of Acts 1:8 activated the spirit of the people in the house. This poured out in Acts 2:1-4 as speaking in tongues, which was the tangible outcome. This inspired a strong witness of preaching or further prophesying by Peter in Acts 2:14-40. The result of it all was people being led to salvation in Acts 2:41.

> *Acts 2 *[40]*With many other words he warned them; and he pleaded with them, "Save yourselves from this corrupt generation."* [41]*Those who accepted his message were baptized, and about three thousand were added to their number that day.*

What God really wants is for people to be saved. That is the most important message of all time! You can be saved.

Salvation is the ultimate goal of a true spiritual move of God.

Therefore, the essence of the message Paul begins in 1 Corinthians 14 is that you should have a stronger desire for the spirit in others to be built up than a desire for your own spiritual enlightening. Prophecy is the key to activating or awakening the spirit in others.

> *1 Corinthians 14 *[1]*Follow the way of love and eagerly desire spiritual gifts, especially the gift of prophecy.* [2]*For anyone who speaks in a tongue does not speak to men but to God. Indeed, no one understands him; he utters mysteries with his spirit.* [3]*But everyone who prophesies speaks to men for their strengthening, encouragement and comfort.*

The spiritual person within you gets activated by the prophetic word of God. It is also the mechanism by which you are introduced to God as a loving Father and Jesus as a caring Savior.

> *Romans 10 *[13]*for, "Everyone who calls on the name of the Lord [everyone whose spirit is activated] will be saved."* [14]*How, then, can they call on the one they have not believed in? And how can they believe in the one of whom they have not heard [they*

have never been prophesied to]? And how can they hear without someone preaching [prophesying] to them? ¹⁵And how can they preach [prophesy] unless they are sent? As it is written, "How beautiful are the feet of those who bring good news [who activate the spiritual man]!" [Revis annotation]

So then, the desire of saved people within the church must be for the spirit of others to be activated by prophecy. Spiritual activation or enlightening must be the goal. Prophesying does this to the good of others as its priority work. Prophecy does not have a self-based motive. Your spirit-filled works should not either.

Philippians 2 ³Do nothing out of selfish ambition or vain conceit, but in humility consider others better than yourselves.

With spiritual awakening comes improved clarity about other moves of God in your life. It becomes clear and evident that God is at work because new life shows up in a real and tangible way. An activated spirit lets you know God intends to bless you. It is the Holy Spirit that lets you believe it and receive it.

1 John 2 ²⁰But you have an anointing [enlightenment, awakening, activation] from the Holy One, and all of you know the truth. [Revis annotation]

The story of Ezekiel in the valley of dry bones is a marvelous example of the power of the prophetic word. It brought about a great move of God. It restored life where there only seemed to be death.

Ezekiel 37 ¹The hand of the LORD was upon me, and he brought me out by the Spirit of the LORD and set me in the middle of a valley; it was full of bones. ²He led me back and forth among them, and I saw a great many bones on the floor of the valley, bones that were very dry. ³He asked me, "Son of man, can these bones live?" I said, "O Sovereign LORD, you alone know." ⁴Then he said to me, "Prophesy to these bones and say to them, 'Dry bones, hear the word of the LORD! ⁵This is what the Sovereign LORD says to these bones: I will make breath enter you, and you will come to life. ⁶I will attach tendons to you and make flesh come upon you and cover you with skin; I will put breath in you, and you will come to life. Then you will know that I am the LORD.'" ⁷So I prophesied as I was commanded. And as I was prophesying, there was a noise, a rattling sound, and the bones came together, bone to bone. ⁸I looked, and tendons and flesh appeared on them and skin covered them, but there was no breath in them. ⁹Then he said to me, "Prophesy to the breath; prophesy, son of man, and say to it, 'This is what the Sovereign LORD says: Come from the four winds, O breath, and breathe into these slain, that they may live.'" ¹⁰So I prophesied as he commanded me, and breath entered them; they came to life and stood up on their feet—a vast army.

Ezekiel was told to prophesy to the dry bones. When he did, a miraculous awakening occurred that brought about a clear, tangible result. This was clearly a move of God! It was a measurable miracle! It was brought about by placing priority on prophecy.

So the prophetic word leads to an activated spirit, which leads to tangible actions and responses. This is what a true spiritual move of God is all about. It is a miraculous and measurable change in the existing conditions and prevailing situations.

Isaiah 55 ¹¹so is my word that goes out from my mouth: It will not return to me empty, but will accomplish what I desire and achieve the purpose for which I sent it.

It must be pointed out that experiencing a spiritual move of God requires faith. It requires the sure expectation that what is believed and prophetically spoken will happen and come to pass.

Faith is also strengthened by the prophetic word of God.

Romans 10 ¹⁷Consequently, faith comes from hearing the message [hearing the prophecy], and the message is heard through the word of Christ. [Revis annotation]

Faith puts you in a position before God to receive the tangible outpouring of His spiritual nature. It is your password to personal interactions with God!

Hebrews 11 ⁶And without faith it is impossible to please God [to interact intimately with God], because anyone who comes to him must believe that he exists [His Spirit can be experienced or touched] and that he rewards those who earnestly seek him. [Revis annotation]

When faith is spoken or prophesied, it demands a measurable outcome. Active faith produces a measurable result. It brings miracles into being.

Matthew 17 ²⁰He replied, "Because you have so little faith. I [Jesus] tell you the truth, if you have faith as small as a mustard seed, you can say [speak, prophecy] to this mountain, 'Move from here to there' and it will move. Nothing will be impossible for you." [Revis annotation]

Notice that Jesus used the word "say," which means speak or prophesy in this context. This lets you know that there is power in the spoken word and spoken prophecy of God. The spoken word of God demands a measurable outcome. A changed life is the ultimate measure of the power of God's word. This is why the prophetic word of God must have a priority position in the church.

Paul did not want the church to lose sight of its true mission. That mission was to help change the lives of people and bring them to repentance before it was too late.

2 Peter 3 ⁹The Lord is not slow in keeping his promise, as some understand slowness. He is patient with you, not wanting anyone to perish, but everyone to come to repentance.

The mission still is to save souls for Christ. To do so, people need to hear a clearly defined, directly understandable word about God. There needs to be no ambiguity in what they hear if change is to result.

1 Corinthians 14 ⁶Now, brothers, if I come to you and speak in tongues, what good will I be to you, unless I bring you some revelation or knowledge or prophecy or word of instruction?

Speaking in tongues at Corinth had become a distraction for the early church. It had divided the Corinthian church. The people had inadvertently shifted emphasis from the prophetic word. The spiritual operations were skewed towards speaking in tongues. Paul sought to restore unity and balance in the spiritual events of the church.

1 Corinthians 1 ¹⁰I appeal to you, brothers, in the name of our Lord Jesus Christ, that all of you agree with one another so that there may be no divisions among you and that you may be perfectly united in mind and thought.

Unfortunately, speaking in tongues is often a distraction for many within the church today. It should not be so. It is clearly not God's intent.

Paul sought to set the record straight on prophecy and speaking in tongues when he wrote his letter to the church at Corinth. The intent was summarized nicely on its own.

1 Corinthians 14 ³⁹Therefore, my brothers, be eager to prophesy, and do not forbid speaking in tongues. ⁴⁰But everything should be done in a fitting and orderly way.

Prophecy is the voice that invites heaven to respond in a tangible way. It also signals that heaven wants to respond with a defined, measurable outpour. In other words, prophecy puts you in touch with heaven's resources and mandates. It connects you to the desires of God.

Prophecy starts in the spirit-mind of God. It is experienced in the physical world of man.

Chapter 5. The Eternal Nature of Prophecy

The prophecies of the past were immediate because they had meaning to the people at that specific time period. But they were also imminent in that they would have meaning to people thereafter, including you and me.

The first prophetic word was spoken by God. It happened on the day of creation. That particular prophetic word has been re-spoken ever since, for good reason. It still brings newness.

> *Genesis 1 ³And God said, "Let there be light," and there was light.*

This first prophetic word came from God. That is a very important and powerful point to note. It means that the prophetic word comes out of the nature of God. And since it comes out of the nature of God, it is just like God. God is eternal, which means His prophetic word is eternal.

> *Psalm 90 ²Before the mountains were born or you brought forth the earth and the world, from everlasting to everlasting you are God.*

Since God is always eternal, it means His prophetic word is always eternal. This is an important spiritual principle to know about God's word. Every word that God has ever spoken is eternal because it comes from His eternal nature. Therefore, like God, His word will never end! Even this was eternally prophesied.

> *Matthew 24 ³⁵Heaven and earth will pass away, but my words will never pass away.*

Perhaps you can understand the eternal nature of the prophetic word even better by recalling first that Jesus and God are fully one.

> *John 10 ³⁰I [Jesus] and my Father are one. [Revis annotation]*

Therefore, when Jesus spoke of Himself, He was also speaking of Himself as God! It all sounds a bit strange at first, but His word says it is true.

John 1 ¹In the beginning was the Word [Jesus, prophecy], and the Word [Jesus, prophecy] was with God, and the Word [Jesus, prophecy] was God. ²The same was in the beginning with God. [Revis annotation]

Prophecy is eternal. This is good news! And since prophecy is eternal, all the prophecies ever spoken have value, even now.

The spiritual outpouring of the previously spoken prophetic words and the works thereof were for a specific time period. Yet, many were forespoken revelations for us right now! The prophecies of the past were immediate because they had meaning to the people at that specific time period. But they were also imminent in that they would have meaning to people thereafter, including you and me.

1 Corinthians 10 ¹¹These things happened to them as examples and were written down as warnings for us, on whom the fulfillment of the ages has come.

The word of God, His prophecy, is alive. The Bible is not a collection of dead strokes of ink on paper. Instead, the Bible is the living, breathing, prophetic gathering of a portion of the known will of God!

Hebrews 4 ¹²For the word of God is living and active. Sharper than any double-edged sword, it penetrates even to dividing soul and spirit, joints and marrow; it judges the thoughts and attitudes of the heart.

Having a living word of God is why the principles of the Old Testament are as valid today as they were when they were written. That is why the New Testament writings did not destroy the Old Testament writings, because God's word is eternal. This makes what Jesus said have even greater meaning.

Matthew 5 ¹⁷Think not that I am come to destroy the law, or the prophets: I am not come to destroy, but to fulfill.

The exact events, ways, mannerisms and idioms of the Old Testament and New Testament cannot always be instituted today. They often cannot because of evolving cultures, social development, world conditions and time-driven technological advances. But the prophetic messages and the principles thereof are unchanged, just as Christ, the living prophecy, is unchanged.

Hebrews 13 [8]Jesus Christ is the same yesterday and today and forever.

Prophecies are the eternal outpouring from the very nature of God. They cannot be destroyed. They cannot be destroyed because they have no fixed beginning or ending. They just are, even as God just is.

Revelation 1 [8]I am Alpha and Omega, the beginning and the ending, saith the Lord, which is, and which was, and which is to come, the Almighty.

Prophecy certainly does have a historical point of reference. That is how we got the Bible. The Bible was collected from the historical records of divinely inspire men and women of God. Each historical event happened at a specific time and place. But the true spiritual origin was beyond that. As a matter of fact, it happened before the authors, many of whom were prophets, knew of their own human existence. The specific prophecy was already known in the eternal spirit-mind of God.

Jeremiah 1 [5] "Before I formed you in the womb I knew you, before you were born I set you apart; I appointed you as a prophet to the nations."

So God's prophecy is eternal because His nature is eternal. Therefore, whatever God said before is good for you today and tomorrow. Fortunately, the core of God's prophecy to man is available in the Holy Bible.

2 Timothy 3 ¹⁶*All Scripture is Godbreathed and is useful for teaching, rebuking, correcting and training in righteousness.*

The Bible is an eternal work of prophecy. It is the spoken knowledge of the very nature of God's innermost being. It is the breath of God.

Psalm 33 ⁶ *By the word of the LORD were the heavens made, their starry host by the breath of his mouth.*

Prophecies and teachings in the Bible are collections of trustworthy and unchangeable principles of God. You get to know God's intentions from the Bible. What you discover is that whatever was spoken before for the good of others has value to you today. That is evidence of its eternal nature.

Prophecy is the eternal word of God that expresses His nature in a way such that man, by faith, can benefit from His wisdom.

Chapter 6. A Priority on Prophecy

It is the responsibility of great prophetic outpourings to make room for more spiritual gifts, not limit them.

Prophecy is God revealing Himself to mankind. It is born out of the very nature of God, which makes it eternal. The eternal revelation of prophecy starts in the spirit of God and manifests itself in a tangible way to man. Something significant happens in the life of the person or the life of the situation when the prophetic word is put forth. The significance is often measured by a miraculous or clear change that is not otherwise possible without God's intervention. This brings special value to the event as God's presence is revealed.

One of the most significant of such events ever recorded happened on the Day of Pentecost in Acts 2. On that day, the baptism of the Holy Spirit was poured out on the Apostles and the other people in Jerusalem. This was the first occurrence of the full outpouring of the Holy Spirit in this manner. It introduced man to a new expression. That expression became known as speaking in tongues, the gift of tongues or simply tongues.

> *Acts 2 ¹When the day of Pentecost came, they [the Apostles] were all together in one place. ²Suddenly a sound like the blowing of a violent wind came from heaven and filled the whole house where they were sitting. ³They saw what seemed to be tongues of fire that separated and came to rest on each of them. [Revis annotation]*

The baptism of the Holy Spirit was prophesied on at least two previous New Testament occasions. It was prophesied by John the Baptist in Luke 3 and by Jesus in Acts 1. This clearly shows the importance and consistency of God's prophetic word.

> *Luke 3 ¹⁶John answered, saying unto them all, I indeed baptize you with water; but one mightier than I cometh, the latchet of whose shoes I am not worthy to unloose: he shall baptize you with the Holy Ghost and with fire.*

> *Acts 1 ⁸But you will receive power when the Holy Spirit comes on you; and you will be my [Jesus] witnesses in Jerusalem, and*

in all Judea and Samaria, and to the ends of the earth. [Revis annotation]

The prophetic word clearly holds a special position within the works of God. This point is well-known to the Christian community. It is undeniable and is rarely debated. After all, God spoke the first prophetic words in the opening verses of Genesis.

Genesis 1 ¹In the beginning God created the heavens and the earth. ²Now the earth was formless and empty, darkness was over the surface of the deep, and the Spirit of God was hovering over the waters. ³And God said, "Let there be light," and there was light.

We find the specifically spoken prophecy in Genesis 1:3. We also see the tangible result.

Genesis 1 ³And God said [prophesied], "Let there be [activate, establish, bring forth, create, build up] light," and there was light [visible, tangible]. [Revis annotation]

Creation started in the spirit-mind of God. It moved to the spoken, prophetic voice of God. It manifested itself in the tangible, physical articles of the world we now live in. What a miracle!

That is why Paul places such a premium on prophecy over the other gifts. All the gifts are important. Never forget this point. All spiritual gifts have value. However, Paul points out in 1 Corinthians 14 that if a choice has to be made with regard to public events, then choose prophecy; because of its eternal nature right from the spirit-heart of God.

The church at Corinth, for reasons that are not altogether evident, found themselves in a situation where Paul felt compelled to make a decision for them with regard to how prophecy and speaking in tongues should occur within the church. It is likely that the selfish and immature motives of the people created the need for Paul's resolution.

1 Corinthians 14 ¹Follow the way of love and eagerly desire spiritual gifts, especially the gift of prophecy.

This statement caused many at that time to misinterpret Paul's intent. It has caused some today to do likewise. Furthermore, the biases that later ensued caused many to miss the truly wonderful wisdom in Paul's mandate. What to some appeared to be a restriction was instead a remarkable show of wisdom.

Psalm 49 ³My mouth will speak words of wisdom; the utterance from my heart will give understanding.

This was an awesome decision to place prophecy as the priority gift, and here is why. Prophecy brings about a tangible blessing that is consistent with the will of God. That is the role of prophecy—to produce a tangible outcome. And one of those tangible outcomes could very well be the gift of tongues!

There was no prohibition on prophecy leading to speaking in tongues. There was simply a warning against the immature, out-of-order expression of tongues.

In some instances, the tangible outcome of prophecy will be the verbal outpouring of speaking in tongues!

That is truly amazing! Prophecy does not eliminate the opportunity for speaking in tongues. It provides for it. Prophecy supports speaking in tongues. Speaking in tongues is one of the natural, tangible outcomes of receiving an impartation of God's prophetic word.

It is inspirational to witness how Paul put things in order without eliminating God's desire for the church to be gifted with speaking in tongues. Understanding that prophecy can lead to speaking in tongues helps to reconcile what seems to be a conflict. It is about priority not superiority. Priority does not require superiority. Placing one gift first does not mean the other is not valued.

At this particular time, which was after Pentecost, the church as a whole was still adjusting to the new influx of spiritual gifts. The Corinthian church was no exception. They were spiritually immature with regard to some spiritual events. So they found themselves with a paradox with regard to prophecy and speaking in tongues. Paul's resolution removed the dilemma by placing the priority on prophecy, which we now know makes room for speaking in tongues!

> **It is the responsibility of great prophetic outpours to make room for more spiritual gifts, not limit them!**

There is a priority on prophecy. There is also synergy between prophecy and speaking in tongues. The synergy works to build up the church by taking advantage of the distinct features of each gift.

> *1 Corinthians 14. ³But everyone who prophesies speaks to men for their strengthening, encouragement and comfort. ⁴He who speaks in a tongue edifies himself, but he who prophesies edifies the church. ⁵I would like every one of you to speak in tongues, but I would rather have you prophesy. He who prophesies is greater than one who speaks in tongues, unless he interprets, so that the church may be edified.*

Prophecy is to the spirit as bread is to the body. Bread builds up the physical body and prophecy builds up the spiritual body. Jesus taught this principle about prophecy to His disciples.

Matthew 4 ⁴Jesus answered, "It is written: 'Man does not live on bread alone, but on every word [prophecy] that comes from the mouth of God.'" [Revis annotation]

The better the quality of your physical bread, the better is your physical health and life. In the same fashion, the better the quality of the prophetic word in your life, the better is your spiritual life.

An improved spiritual life is a key tangible outcome of the prophetic word. Always remember that one of the works of prophecy is to activate the spirit. Therefore, you should expect change when you hear the preaching of the gospel.

So Paul is not teaching against speaking in tongues in 1 Corinthians 14. He is placing the gifts of prophecy and tongues in order, allowing them to operate in synergy.

Speaking in tongues clearly is a spiritual gift that exists to benefit the church. Prophecy makes room for it.

Prophecy has the priority for good reasons. It is the preferred spiritual choice. But this does not mean hearing tongues openly spoken in the church assembly is always out of order. Paul did not intend to suggest that the church should be void of speaking in tongues. This does not seem reasonable, especially when you consider Paul also spoke in tongues.

1 Corinthians 14 ¹⁸I [Paul] thank God that I speak in tongues more than all of you. [Revis annotation]

So even with the priority on prophecy, hearing tongues spoken in the church is not automatically out of order. Paul said so.

1 Corinthians 14 ³⁹Therefore, my brothers, be eager to prophesy, and do not forbid speaking in tongues.

In addition, speaking in tongues might also well be in order by the permission of the overseer or pastor of the church as the shepherd.

Jeremiah 3 ¹⁵Then I will give you shepherds after my own heart, who will lead you with knowledge and understanding.

Also, on occasion, the spirit will overrun the discipline of one's physical control. When it does, a legitimate physical response in tongues might happen. Then, speaking in tongues might spontaneously come out! Withholding the expression of tongues at such a moment would obviously be against the spoken wishes of the Holy Spirit.

1 Thessalonians 5 ¹⁹Do not put out the Spirit's fire.

In other words, speaking in tongues just might come out because of an overflow of the spirit. This cannot completely be stopped or overruled, even in the most disciplined believer.

Luke 6 ⁴⁵The good man brings good things out of the good stored up in his heart, and the evil man brings evil things out of the evil stored up in his heart. For out of the overflow [spiritual overflow] of his heart his mouth speaks [tongues in some instances]. [Revis annotation]

Paul did not teach against speaking in tongues in 1 Corinthian 14. Instead, he instructed the church to have discipline and maturity in the use of all gifts, including speaking in tongues. He set the priority of speaking in tongues after prophecy with regard to public assembly.

1 Corinthians 14 ¹⁹But in the church [during public assembly for prayer and worship] I would rather speak five intelligible words to instruct others than ten thousand words in a tongue. [Revis annotation]

Paul pointed out that there should be discipline in the priority and expression of spiritual gifts. The discipline should be at the dictate of the Holy Spirit. The Holy Spirit should be the guide for prophecy and speaking in tongues. They are both precious gifts of the spirit, even though prophecy has the priority.

Chapter 7. Paul's Personal Position

Paul's speaking in tongues was several years after Pentecost. If Pentecost was the only time for speaking in tongues, then what was Paul doing?

Paul was the prophetic author of a great portion of the New Testament. He was a well respected, ordained authority on God's design for the church. As a matter of fact, he founded the church at Corinth as an apostle.

> *1 Corinthians 9 ²Even though I may not be an apostle to others, surely I am to you! For you are the seal of my apostleship in the Lord.*

Apostle Paul was also the father of many other churches throughout Asia Minor during his lifetime. His impeccable record for Jesus Christ as an apostle, pastor and teacher speaks for itself.

> *2 Timothy 1 ¹¹And of this gospel I was appointed a herald and an apostle and a teacher.*

Paul's greatness and value to the work of the church was spoken of by the Lord. And his selection as an apostle is unquestionable. He was called to evangelize much of the early Christian world.

> *Acts 9 ¹⁵But the Lord said to Ananias, "Go! This man is my chosen instrument to carry my name before the Gentiles and their kings and before the people of Israel.*

Paul was fervent in the service of the Lord ever since his miraculous conversion on the road to Damascus. On that day, Paul personally met the Lord Jesus Christ and was saved by grace. He continued to testify about his miraculous change for years to come.

> *Acts 22 ⁶"About noon as I came near Damascus, suddenly a bright light from heaven flashed around me. ⁷I fell to the ground and heard a voice say to me, 'Saul! Saul! Why do you persecute me?' ⁸"'Who are you, Lord?' I asked. " 'I am Jesus of Nazareth, whom you are persecuting,' he replied. ⁹My companions saw the light, but they did not understand the voice of him who was speaking to me. ¹⁰ "'What shall I do, Lord?' I asked. "'Get up,' the Lord said,*

'and go into Damascus. There you will be told all that you have been assigned to do.'

There was one other thing this great man of God did after being saved. Paul spoke in tongues. It is not clear exactly when he began to speak. But the Bible is very clear on the fact that he did.

1 Corinthians 14 ¹⁸I thank God that I [Paul] speak in tongues more than all of you. [Revis annotation]

Paul's first encounter with speaking in tongues could have happened during the visit of Ananias, shortly after Paul's conversion on the road to Damascus.

Acts 9 ¹⁷Then Ananias went to the house and entered it. Placing his hands on Saul, he said, "Brother Saul, the Lord—Jesus, who appeared to you on the road as you were coming here—has sent me so that you may see again and be filled with the Holy Spirit." ¹⁸Immediately, something like scales fell from Saul's eyes, and he could see again. He got up and was baptized [water or Holy Spirit], ¹⁹and after taking some food, he regained his strength. [Revis annotation]

The timing of when Paul received the baptism of the Holy Spirit with speaking in tongues is somewhat ambiguous. But it is clear that speaking in tongues was part of his life.

1 Corinthians 14 ¹⁸I thank God that I speak in tongues more than all of you.

Paul said, I "speak" in tongues. He did not say he thought in tongues. Neither did he say he meditated in tongues. He clearly stated that a verbal expression came from his lips. He called the expression speaking in tongues.

Notice also that Paul used the present tense "speak." He did not say he "spoke" in tongues or once spoke in tongues and then stopped. Paul said he was presently speaking in tongues.

Paul was speaking in tongues in his present time. This point is worth consideration by those who hold that speaking in tongues both started and stopped at Pentecost. Paul's speaking in tongues was several years after Pentecost. If Pentecost was the only time for speaking in tongues, then what was Paul doing? Was he caught up in emotional exuberance as some would say about other believers? I doubt it. Paul was acting under the baptism of the Holy Spirit.

Paul was presently, in his time, earnestly involved in a spiritual event. That event was called speaking in tongues. Therefore, speaking in tongues had not ceased at the time of Paul.

It is further clear that speaking in tongues had not ceased during the time of Paul when you consider 1 Corinthians 13:8.

1 Corinthians 13 [8]Love never fails. But where there are prophecies, they will cease; where there are tongues, they will be stilled; where there is knowledge, it will pass away.

Paul says of tongues that "they will be stilled." This means the gift of tongues certainly will stop someday. But because his statement includes the word "will," it means they had not yet done so. And to my knowledge, there are no teachings after Paul's that say they did. Therefore, it seems prudent to believe they still exist as promised.

Acts 2 [39]The promise is for you and your children and for all who are far off—for all whom the Lord our God will call.

One other comment is noteworthy with regard to 1 Corinthians 13:8. The "prophecies, they will cease" does not mean those already spoken prophecies will become invalid. The spoken prophecies to date will come true and have impact. The phrase "prophecies, they will cease" means there will come a time when the prophetic word of God in the earth will end. This will be at the final end-time reign of the Lord, which is yet to come.

> *Revelation 19 ⁶Then I heard what sounded like a great multitude, like the roar of rushing waters and like loud peals of thunder, shouting: "Hallelujah! For our Lord God Almighty reigns."*

Paul was an apostle of Jesus Christ. This means he was divinely called by God to specifically establish foundational principles by which the church was to live out its spiritual life. He was also called to correct and abolish any actions within the church that were out of order with God. His letter in 1 Corinthians 14 was a perfect opportunity for him to clearly do away with speaking in tongues. But he did not.

Speaking in tongues was a spiritual expression that Paul was participating in. It would be unlikely that he would have taught against it.

Chapter 8. Synergy of Prophecy and Tongues

People are saved by hearing the prophetic word of God. They are empowered to witness by the baptism of the Holy Spirit. The baptism of the Holy Spirit is evidenced by speaking in tongues.

It is clear by Paul's introductory verses in 1 Corinthians 14 that prophecy, or anointed preaching of the gospel, should have priority over other gifts. More specifically, Paul points out that prophecy must supersede speaking in tongues in times of choice during public assembly. But nowhere in his discourse does Paul say to completely abolish speaking in tongues. Read it for yourself.

> *1 Corinthians 14 [1]Follow the way of love and eagerly desire spiritual gifts, especially the gift of prophecy. [2]For anyone who speaks in a tongue does not speak to men but to God. Indeed, no one understands him; he utters mysteries with his spirit. [3]But everyone who prophesies speaks to men for their strengthening, encouragement and comfort. [4]He who speaks in a tongue edifies himself, but he who prophesies edifies the church. [5]I would like every one of you to speak in tongues, but I would rather have you prophesy. He who prophesies is greater than one who speaks in tongues, unless he interprets, so that the church may be edified.*

Prophecy and speaking in tongues are two spiritual gifts to the church. Prophecy is eternal and speaking in tongues is not yet abolished. Therefore, it is important for us to understand the relationship between the two gifts so we can gain the best value God intends for us.

There is clear, anointed synergy between prophecy and speaking in tongues. Once properly viewed, it will cause even the greatest skeptics among believers to rethink their biased positions about spiritual gifts to the church, especially speaking in tongues.

Let us start to uncover the synergy of prophecy and tongues by examining a portion of Acts 19. The events of this passage happened at the town of Ephesus, almost twenty years after Pentecost. Read it with a fresh mind towards hearing God speak directly to you through His prophetic word.

> *Acts 19 [1]While Apollos was at Corinth, Paul took the road through the interior and arrived at Ephesus. There he found some disciples [2]and asked them, "Did you receive the Holy Spirit when you*

believed?" They answered, "No, we have not even heard that there is a Holy Spirit." ³So Paul asked, "Then what baptism did you receive?" "John's baptism," they replied. ⁴Paul said, "John's baptism was a baptism of repentance. He told the people to believe in the one coming after him, that is, in Jesus." ⁵On hearing this, they were baptized into the name of the Lord Jesus. ⁶When Paul placed his hands on them, the Holy Spirit came on them, and they spoke in tongues and prophesied.

Speaking in tongues was happening almost twenty years after the outpouring on the Day of Pentecost. Its value was being taught by Paul. He encouraged the people to receive it, which they did.

With regard to water baptism, it clearly came before baptism of the Holy Spirit. So water baptism was clearly not the same event as baptism of the Holy Spirit. Instead, water baptism was traditionally called the baptism of John unto repentance. It was an important act of righteousness used to signify a person had been converted to the way of Jesus Christ, which we now know as becoming a Christian or being saved.

Acts 11 ²⁶...The disciples were called Christians first at Antioch.

The Ephesians were saved because of their belief in Jesus Christ. This came by hearing the prophetic word of God. So their salvation came after hearing the gospel, but before water baptism. It also came before baptism of the Holy Spirit, with evidence of speaking in tongues. So salvation unmistakably comes before water baptism and the gift of spiritual tongues.

Being saved, however, does not necessarily mean a person receives the gift of tongues. Salvation does not guarantee gifting of any sort. Look again at the Acts 19:2 account.

Acts 19 [2]and asked them, "Did you receive the Holy Spirit when you believed?" They answered, "No, we have not even heard that there is a Holy Spirit."

Notice that Paul asked, "Did you receive the Holy Spirit when you believed?" "Believed" means the Ephesians were already saved. But they had not yet received the gift of speaking in tongues. As a matter of fact, they did not know it was possible for them to have the gift of tongues.

It is unfortunate, even after the many trustworthy biblical accounts and prophetic messages, that some believers today still do not know the gift of tongues is available to them. Then there are others who believe it is available, but are failing to "eagerly" seek it as instructed by Apostle Paul.

1 Corinthians 14 [1]... eagerly desire spiritual gifts...

We also learn from Acts 19:1-6 that baptism of the Holy Spirit, with evidence of speaking in tongues, does not necessarily accompany salvation or water baptism. It certainly did not accompany either event for the Ephesians. Recall that Paul was talking to believers. These people were saved.

Acts 19 [2]and asked them, "Did you receive the Holy Spirit when you believed?

Speaking in tongues is a specifically dispensed gift from God. It is not an automatic allowance of salvation. In other words, you can be perfectly saved and not receive the gift of tongues by baptism of the Holy Spirit.

So speaking in tongues happens upon the specific baptism of the Holy Spirit in the life of a believer; a born-again Christian. Being born again is the single most important requirement.

John 3 ⁷You should not be surprised at my [Jesus] saying, 'You must be born again.' [Revis annotation]

Only born-again believers can speak in tongues after baptism of the Holy Spirit.

Baptism of the Holy Spirit in this specific manner does not bring salvation. This is clearly revealed by the Acts 19:1-6 account, as already discussed.

Baptism of the Holy Spirit authorizes power-packed gifting from heaven. Notice what Acts 1:8 says.

Acts 1 ⁸But you will receive power [ability, authority] when the Holy Spirit comes on [baptizes] you; and you will be my witnesses in Jerusalem, and in all Judea and Samaria, and to the ends of the earth." [Revis annotation]

Acts 1:8 is a very strong prophetic word. It says you will definitely receive the power to be an effective witness "when the Holy Spirit comes upon you." This means when the Holy Spirit baptizes you.

This prophecy was fulfilled, based on the report of salvation in Acts 2:40-46. In other words, the effectiveness of the apostles' witness was magnified by their baptism of the Holy Spirit.

Acts 2 ⁴⁰With many other words he warned them; and he pleaded with them, "Save yourselves from this corrupt generation." ⁴¹Those who accepted his message were baptized, and about three thousand were added to their number [saved] that day. [Revis annotation]

Acts 2 ⁴⁶Every day they continued to meet together in the temple courts. They broke bread in their homes and ate together with glad and sincere hearts, ⁴⁷praising God and enjoying the favor of all the people. And the Lord added [tangible response] to their number [the church] daily those who were being saved [believing the preaching of the gospel]. [Revis annotation]

The synergy between prophecy and speaking in tongues is the mechanism by which God deposits tangible outcomes in the church. Together they build up the church. People are saved by hearing the prophetic word of God. They are empowered to witness by the baptism of the Holy Spirit. The baptism of the Holy Spirit is evidenced by speaking in tongues.

Chapter 9. Who Can Speak in Tongues

Where there is no salvation, there can be no speaking in tongues. Speaking in tongues without salvation is false pretense.

After His resurrection and just prior to His ascension back to heaven, Jesus told His disciples to expect a miraculous change in their lives. The change would give them the power and authority to be effective witnesses throughout the world.

> *Acts 1 ⁸But you will receive power when the Holy Spirit comes on you; and you will be my witnesses in Jerusalem, and in all Judea and Samaria, and to the ends of the earth."*

This scripture says you will receive "power" after the Holy Spirit comes on you, which means baptizes you. It does not say you will receive "salvation." It specifically says you will receive power. The word "power" cannot be confused in any translation or language with the word salvation.

Therefore, Acts 1:8 is not talking about receiving salvation. It is talking about receiving the authorized power to witness effectively.

Acts 1:8 supports the position that baptism of the Holy Spirit does not necessarily bring salvation. Salvation must already be present in a person who receives the gift of tongues—not the opposite! In other words, speaking in tongues does not lead to salvation. Speaking in tongues is a gift after salvation. It testifies of having the anointed power to witness.

Salvation is clearly and unquestionably by the grace of God. It happens because of belief in Jesus Christ. It is not by any other means.

> *Ephesians 2 ⁸For it is by grace you have been saved, through faith–and this not from yourselves, it is the gift of God– ⁹not by works, so that no one can boast.*

The Ephesians 2:8 scripture does not say you are saved by baptism of Holy Spirit. It does not say you are saved by speaking in tongues. It says you are saved by grace.

Ephesians 2:8 goes on to say, "not from yourselves" and "not by works." This means salvation does not happen by any action on your part.

Think about it. Speaking in tongues would be an action. Therefore, speaking in tongues cannot be required for salvation.

It is clear that salvation stands on its own unearned favor of God's grace. It does not happen by any action other than belief. It is likewise clear that salvation is necessary before one can receive the gift of speaking in tongues.

Therefore, unsaved people do not receive the spiritual gift of speaking in tongues. Speaking in tongues is a power-built blessing from God for those who will be witnesses for Him. Only saved people want to witness for the Lord. Saved people are the only ones capable of a true witness. Therefore, do not expect the unsaved to speak in tongues. It cannot happen.

The hard truth is that some people will never speak in tongues because they are not saved.

Unsaved people have great testimonies about their lives. And some are even very inspirational. But the testimony of an unsaved person is rarely for the specific purpose of inviting others to Jesus Christ. Believers are the ones specifically called to the life-long duty of being Christ's witnesses. Believers are the only ones who know the truth about who God really is.

John 8 [31]To the Jews who had believed him, Jesus said, "If you hold to my teaching, you are really my disciples. [32]Then you will know the truth, and the truth will set you free."

So the unsaved cannot speak in tongues. This is one reason it should concern a saved person who sincerely desires to speak in tongues, but does not yet. The question of whether they are saved should come to mind.

It may be a tough question to face for some. But you should ask yourself whether you are saved if you have earnestly sought baptism of the Holy Spirit and have not yet received it! It does not automatically mean that you are not saved. But it certainly should be considered. And if you are unsure about your salvation, right now is the best time to ask the Lord into your life.

Romans 10 [13]for, "Everyone who calls on the name of the Lord will be saved."

Let me put it to you very simply. Where there is no salvation, there can be no speaking in tongues. Speaking in tongues without salvation is false pretense.

There might be those who pretend to speak in tongues or who get caught up in emotionalism. However, their actions do not negate the fact that speaking in tongues has genuinely happened in the lives of many true believers.

So not being saved is one reason some do not receive the baptism of the Holy Spirit. They cannot, because the gift is intended for saved people. It is reserved for believers.

One other reason why some might not have received the baptism of the Holy Spirit is because of their lack of knowledge. The new converts in Acts 19 faced this situation. So Apostle Paul educated them. He prophesied to them about the power of being baptized with the Holy Spirit.

Acts 19 [1]While Apollos was at Corinth, Paul took the road through the interior and arrived at Ephesus. There he found some disciples [2]and asked them, "Did you receive the Holy Spirit when you believed?" They answered, "No, we have not even heard that there is a Holy Spirit." [3]So Paul asked, "Then what baptism did you receive?" "John's baptism," they replied. [4]Paul said, "John's baptism was a baptism of repentance. He told the people to believe in the one coming after him, that is, in Jesus.

Paul educated the people at Ephesus about what was available to them. They essentially received an informed, prophetic word. Remember that prophecy activates the spirit to bring about a true, tangible response. In this instance, the tangible outcome was the verbal gift of tongues.

Acts 19 ⁵On hearing this, they were baptized into the name of the Lord Jesus. ⁶When Paul placed his hands on them, the Holy Spirit came on them, and they spoke in tongues and prophesied.

Paul did not teach the Ephesians how to speak in tongues. No one can do that. True speaking in tongues is a gift, not a learned religious exercise.

Instead, Paul taught the Ephesian believers about the availability of the gift of tongues to them. He evidently did so with a strong sense of prophetic conviction. After this, Paul laid hands on them and they received the gift of tongues; and they also prophesied.

Paul's convicting prophecy led to speaking in tongues. That prophecy was consistent with the prophecy of Jesus in Acts 1:8.

Acts 1 ⁸But you will receive power when the Holy Spirit comes on you; and you will be my witnesses in Jerusalem, and in all Judea and Samaria, and to the ends of the earth.

Note that this prophecy by Jesus was also recorded in Mark with similar emphasis.

Mark 16 ¹⁷And these signs will accompany those who believe: In my name they will drive out demons; they will speak in new tongues.

Jesus said believers would speak in new tongues, meaning people who were saved. So speaking in tongues was prophesied by Jesus to be a gift for people who were already saved!

Prophecy is eternal. The events of Acts 1 and Acts 2 are simply re-prophesying what Jesus previously spoke in Mark 16 and what Joel spoke in Joel 2. The prophecy was living and looking for its time to become tangible. It found its time at Pentecost.

The prophetic work had gone out from the mouth of Jesus in the book of Mark. His voice placed a spirit in the atmosphere that was re-deposited in believers as a tangible outcome at Pentecost. The outcome was speaking in tongues on the Day of Pentecost. This was an awesome move of God!

> *Acts 2 ¹When the day of Pentecost came, they were all together in one place. ²Suddenly a sound like the blowing of a violent wind came from heaven and filled the whole house where they were sitting. ³They saw what seemed to be tongues of fire that separated and came to rest on each of them. ⁴All of them were filled with the Holy Spirit and began to speak in other tongues as the Spirit enabled them.*

This was not the only time the prophetic word brought about the tangible outcome of speaking in tongues from believers by baptism of the Holy Spirit. There were several occasions reported in the Bible. Consider, for example, Peter's ministry in Acts 10, which was about ten years after Pentecost.

> *Acts 10 ⁴⁴While Peter was still speaking these words, the Holy Spirit came on all who heard the message. ⁴⁵The circumcised believers who had come with Peter were astonished that the gift of the Holy Spirit had been poured out even on the Gentiles.*

Acts 10:44 plainly shows that Peter began speaking, preaching or prophesying to the people after his encounter with the Holy Spirit. As he did, the baptism of the Holy Spirit overtook all the believing listeners. The reason others knew it was the baptism of the Holy Spirit was because they heard people speaking in tongues! This was the tangible outcome of a specific, spiritual move of God on the lives of believing listeners.

> *Acts 10* [46]*For they heard them speaking in tongues and praising God.*

The act of speaking in tongues is for believers. It is not a generic gift to the general world population. Therefore, the unsaved cannot receive the gift. And even when the lack of knowledge and doubt hinders the gift of tongues from manifesting itself within believers, it is still their gift, nonetheless.

Chapter 10. The Salvation Connection

Being saved and having the gift of tongues are not the same things. They are scripturally and spiritually distinct events.

The Apostle Paul clarified in 1 Corinthians 14 how the gift of prophecy and speaking in tongues should work in synergy. He pointed out that prophecy should have the priority position with regard to open expression within the church. Prophecy activates the spirit to seek change.

1 Corinthians 14 ¹Follow the way of love and eagerly desire spiritual gifts, especially the gift of prophecy.

1 Corinthians 14 ³But everyone who prophesies speaks to men for their strengthening, encouragement and comfort.

Speaking in tongues is a gift that builds up the spiritual aptitude of a believer. In building up the individual, speaking in tongues obviously strengthens the church body as a whole. There is no prohibition on speaking in tongues in the church when it works in harmony with prophecy and interpretation.

1 Corinthians 14 ²For anyone who speaks in a tongue does not speak to men but to God. Indeed, no one understands him; he utters mysteries with his spirit. ³But everyone who prophesies speaks to men for their strengthening, encouragement and comfort. ⁴He who speaks in a tongue edifies himself, but he who prophesies edifies the church. ⁵I would like every one of you to speak in tongues, but I would rather have you prophesy. He who prophesies is greater than one who speaks in tongues, unless he interprets, so that the church may be edified.

In 1 Corinthians 14:5, Paul specifically says he would like for all of the members of the Corinthian church to speak in tongues. So Paul obviously believes speaking in tongues has value in the lives of saved people.

At this point, Paul could have easily dismissed speaking in tongues as being nonsense. But he did not! Rather, he clarified its use so it could bring the best benefit to the church. That is what God wants for any of the gifts.

Unfortunately, the gift of tongues has been so badly misunderstood that many within the body of Christ shy away from it. In addition, there are those with the gift who tend to be intolerant of those without it. This is not the proper attitude of faith-filled believers either.

Romans 14 ¹Accept him whose faith is weak, without passing judgment on disputable matters.

One matter that has contributed to misunderstandings about spiritual gifts is the confusion between speaking in tongues and salvation. Specifically, some have alleged that speaking in tongues is synonymous with being saved. They equate salvation to mean speaking in tongues.

So let me set the true biblical record straight. Speaking in tongues is not the same as salvation.

> **Being saved and having the gift of tongues are not the same things. They are scripturally and spiritually distinct events.**

The Bible is very clear on what it takes to be saved. You cannot mistake its message on salvation.

John 3 ¹⁶"For God so loved the world that he gave his one and only Son, that whoever believes in him shall not perish but have eternal life. ¹⁷For God did not send his Son into the world to condemn the world, but to save the world through him.

Romans 10 ¹³for, "Everyone who calls on the name of the Lord will be saved."

Ephesians 2 ⁸For it is by grace you have been saved, through faith—and this not from yourselves, it is the gift of God— ⁹not by works, so that no one can boast.

Titus 2 [11]For the grace of God that brings salvation has appeared to all men.

Salvation clearly is by God's grace, through belief in Jesus Christ. There is no other way. There is absolutely no mention in the Bible where speaking in tongues or any other spiritual gift grants salvation. On this point, we must be absolutely clear. Salvation is the act of God's unearned favor that we call grace.

Ephesians 2 [8]For it is by grace you have been saved, through faith—and this not from yourselves, it is the gift of God.

We receive the grace of salvation through accepting the work of Jesus Christ. We must believe in Jesus to be saved. His name alone brings salvation.

Acts 4 [12]Salvation is found in no one else, for there is no other name [Jesus] under heaven given to men by which we must be saved. [Revis annotation]

Salvation is a free gift of God's grace. Make no mistake about it. However, this does not mean there are no connections between salvation, prophecy and speaking in tongues. There are clear connections.

For example, prophecy is a gift that invites people to receive salvation. That makes for a very valuable connection of prophecy to salvation. This is perhaps another reason Paul put emphasis on prophecy or preaching of the gospel as the priority gift. Prophecy proclaims God's word to all and invites the unsaved to salvation.

Romans 10 [14]How, then, can they call on the one they have not believed in? And how can they believe in the one of whom they have not heard? And how can they hear without someone preaching [prophesying] to them? [Revis annotation]

Likewise, the gift of tongues has a clear connection to salvation. Speaking in tongues is a gift that is available only to those who are saved. In other words, saved people are the only ones who can speak in the true spiritual gift of tongues.

Again, speaking in tongues is clearly linked to salvation. However, this does not mean speaking in tongues will happen automatically upon being saved. Salvation and speaking in tongues do not always happen at the same time. Evidence of this can be seen by considering the Acts 19 account of Paul's travels to Ephesus.

> *Acts 19 ¹While Apollos was at Corinth, Paul took the road through the interior and arrived at Ephesus. There he found some disciples ²and asked them, "Did you receive the Holy Spirit when you believed?" They answered, "No, we have not even heard that there is a Holy Spirit." ³So Paul asked, "Then what baptism did you receive?" "John's baptism," they replied. ⁴Paul said, "John's baptism was a baptism of repentance. He told the people to believe in the one coming after him, that is, in Jesus." ⁵On hearing this, they were baptized into the name of the Lord Jesus. ⁶When Paul placed his hands on them, the Holy Spirit came on them, and they spoke in tongues and prophesied.*

So being saved does not require speaking in tongues. You can be saved without speaking in tongues. However, you can become saved and be baptized in the Holy Spirit, with evidence of speaking in tongues, at about the same time. But salvation is an independent event that must come first!

Now I do not want to sound like I am saying a born-again believer who does not yet speak in tongues should be satisfied without tongues. In no way is that my intent! It is quite the contrary. A believer should be somewhat uncomfortable about his or her walk with the Lord in salvation if he or she has not received the gift of tongues, particularly after seeking it.

You can be saved without speaking in tongues. Make absolutely no mistake about this spiritual fact. But you will need more once you are saved. You will need power to function as an effective witness. You will need more to keep your own spirit refreshed in the love of Christ. Speaking in tongues can bring it to you.

Your relationship with God is a deeply rooted, spiritual relationship. There is no other way to make personal contact with God other than by the spirit. Spiritual contact with God brings intimacy to the relationship between you and Him.

> *John 4 ²⁴God is spirit, and his worshipers must worship in spirit and in truth.*

You can experience a spiritually intimate relationship with God by several means. This spiritual relationship is fundamental to one's life as a believer. The Bible speaks freely of the power and miraculous wonder of such a relationship with God.

> *Psalm 21 ⁶ Surely you have granted him eternal blessings and made him glad with the joy of your presence.*

A spiritual relationship with God works out miracles for you. It puts you in a position to see more clearly the implications of what God wants to do in your life. You see God active in your life and you see tangible results of His intervention and involvement. You experience His intimacy as a personable God. Furthermore, a spiritual relationship opens your mind to the prophetic move of God just like it did for the prophets of the past. You expect to hear from God.

> *Revelation 1 ¹⁰On the Lord's Day I [Apostle John] was in the Spirit, and I heard behind me a loud voice like a trumpet. [Revis annotation]*

> *Ezekiel 11 ¹ Then the Spirit lifted me [Prophet Elijah] up and brought me to the gate of the house of the LORD that faces east. There at the entrance to the gate were twenty-five men, and I saw*

among them Jaazaniah son of Azzur and Pelatiah son of Benaiah, leaders of the people. [Revis annotation]

One of the unique ways of experiencing spiritual intimacy with God is by speaking in tongues. Speaking in tongues puts you in direct contact with the personal nature of God. You literally sit in His holiness.

1 Corinthians 14 ²For anyone who speaks in a tongue does not speak to men but to God. Indeed, no one understands him; he utters mysteries with his spirit.

So spiritual gifting and spiritual relationships are fundamental to interacting with God. It is through the spirit that we come to know we are saved. This makes us God's children and heirs to very specific family promises.

Romans 8 ¹⁶The Spirit himself testifies with our spirit that we are God's children. ¹⁷Now if we are children, then we are heirs—heirs of God and co-heirs with Christ, if indeed we share in his sufferings in order that we may also share in his glory.

Therefore, it should concern you when you have a spiritual relationship with such an awesome God, but He has not shared one of His most precious spiritual gifts with you. This should particularly concern you since you know God wants to lavish gifts and blessings upon you.

1 John 3 ¹How great is the love the Father has lavished on us, that we should be called children of God! And that is what we are! The reason the world does not know us is that it did not know him.

Speaking in tongues is a very precious gift that God wants to shower upon you. God loves you as His child and wants to openly show it. Therefore, you should want spiritual gifts, just as Paul recommended.

1 Corinthians 14 ¹Follow the way of love and eagerly desire spiritual gifts, especially the gift of prophecy.

1 Corinthians 14 ³⁹Therefore, my brothers, be eager to prophesy, and do not forbid speaking in tongues.

Speaking in tongues is a wonderful gift, which you can have after salvation. It is God's special impartation for a spiritual connection to His presence. He gives it exclusively to those who are His saved children.

Speaking in tongues is not given to the unsaved. It is too precious for God to dispense it on those who are not yet His own.

Matthew 7 ⁶"Do not give dogs what is sacred; do not throw your pearls to pigs. If you do, they may trample them under their feet, and then turn and tear you to pieces.

So God does not give the gift of tongues as an empowering gift to the unsaved world. This might be why some believers might question whether a person who does not speak in tongues is saved; since the unsaved cannot speak in tongues.

Again, the Ephesus account of speaking in tongues in Acts 19 shows that being saved and speaking in tongues do not necessarily happen at the same time. Neither do they have to happen within a close time period. It might be better for the body of Christ if the two events did happen close together. But there can be a time gap between them.

There are many wonderful gifts from God that are available to believers. If you are saved, you should want to experience them, including the gift of tongues. Speaking in tongues is not the same as being saved. But speaking in tongues is available to enrich you if you are saved.

Hebrews 6 ⁹Even though we speak like this [in distress], dear friends, we are confident of better things in your [believers, saved] case—things [such as prophecy and tongues] that accompany salvation. [Revis annotation].

Chapter 11. The Baptism at Pentecost

What happened as a result of the Day of Pentecost were three of the greatest events in the history of Christianity.

The Day of Pentecost in Acts 2 was truly a unique outpouring of the Holy Spirit. This is when speaking in tongues began its expression on earth.

Acts 2 ¹When the day of Pentecost came, they were all together in one place. ²Suddenly a sound like the blowing of a violent wind came from heaven and filled the whole house where they were sitting. ³They saw what seemed to be tongues of fire that separated and came to rest on each of them. ⁴All of them were filled with the Holy Spirit and began to speak in other tongues as the Spirit enabled them.

Acts 2 ³⁷When the people heard this, they were cut to the heart and said to Peter and the other apostles, "Brothers, what shall we do?" ³⁸Peter replied, "Repent and be baptized, every one of you, in the name of Jesus Christ for the forgiveness of your sins. And you will receive the gift of the Holy Spirit. ³⁹The promise is for you and your children and for all who are far off–for all whom the Lord our God will call." ⁴⁰With many other words he warned them; and he pleaded with them, "Save yourselves from this corrupt generation." ⁴¹Those who accepted his message were baptized, and about three thousand were added to their number that day.

Acts 2:2 says the Holy Spirit "filled the whole house." Some would argue this means filled all the people, which was reported to be slightly over one hundred twenty. Others would say the Holy Spirit filled only the remaining eleven disciples plus the new addition, who became the first apostles.

It is difficult with the limited scripture to be too specific about whether it was everyone in the room or only the disciples that were initially baptized in the Holy Spirit, with evidence of speaking in tongues. But there are some helpful scripture to consider as you think about it.

In this regard, it appears that there were only believers in the room. This is important towards finding an answer to how many were baptized. Read the following and note particularly Acts 1:15.

Acts 1 [12]Then they returned to Jerusalem from the hill called the Mount of Olives, a Sabbath day's walk from the city. [13]When they arrived, they went upstairs to the room where they were staying. Those present were Peter, John, James and Andrew; Philip and Thomas, Bartholomew and Matthew; James son of Alphaeus and Simon the Zealot, and Judas son of James. [14]They all joined together constantly in prayer, along with the women and Mary the mother of Jesus, and with his brothers. [15]In those days Peter stood up among the believers (a group numbering about a hundred and twenty) [16]and said, "Brothers, the Scripture had to be fulfilled which the Holy Spirit spoke long ago through the mouth of David concerning Judas, who served as guide for those who arrested Jesus— [17]he was one of our number and shared in this ministry."

There were only believers in the room as Acts 1:15 states. This would be expected since evidently one purpose for the meeting was to elect a new member to make up the council of twelve disciples. Since they were all believers, they could have all been saved; even though we do not know the date of their full conversion. This would make them eligible for the gift of tongues; since the baptism of the Holy Spirit, with speaking in tongues, is for saved people. So Acts 2:2 could mean the entire one hundred twenty plus the disciples spoke in tongues. This would be in perfect harmony with scriptural principles about speaking in tongues.

Now the Bible does not unambiguously say when the eleven original disciples in the room were saved. But it seems reasonable that they were saved prior to the Acts 1 meeting. In this regard, John 20 is insightful.

John 20 [18]Mary Magdalene went to the disciples with the news: "I have seen the Lord!" And she told them that he had said these things to her. [19]On the evening of that first day of the week, when the disciples were together, with the doors locked for fear of the Jews, Jesus came and stood among them and said, "Peace be with you!" [20]After he said this, he showed them his hands and side. The disciples were overjoyed when they saw the Lord. [21]Again Jesus said, "Peace be with you! As the Father has sent me, I am sending you." [22]*And with that he breathed on them and said, "Receive the Holy Spirit."*

This event occurred after the resurrection of Jesus from the grave. The Bible clearly says Jesus "breathed on them and said, 'receive the Holy Spirit.'" This was when the indwelling presence of the Holy Spirit brought true salvation by grace to these disciples, who now believed that Jesus was the authentic son of God. Jesus' resurrection from the grave proved His divinity and Lordship beyond their previous doubts. They now accepted Jesus fully as Lord.

So whenever the salvation happened for the disciples and the one hundred twenty, it preceded the Day of Pentecost's event of speaking in tongues. Therefore, whatever numbers were baptized in the room, on the Day of Pentecost, were saved. It certainly included the original disciples, minus Judas. It likely also included the one hundred twenty others.

As a related note, the John 20:22 event is why it is difficult to conceive that Judas was saved before his death. It is likely that Judas was not. In other words, Judas was not present with Jesus and the other disciples after the resurrection. He was not there when Jesus "breathed on them." He missed this key life-changing encounter with Jesus Christ to be filled with the indwelling presence of the Holy Spirit, which would have brought him salvation.

At Pentecost, speaking in tongues was followed by prophetic preaching of the gospel. This led to salvation in the lives of many other listeners. Salvation was followed by baptism.

Acts 2 [41]*Those who accepted his message were baptized, and about three thousand were added to their number that day.*

Notice that Acts 2:41 says only that the listeners were "baptized" and added to the church. It does not explicitly say they were baptized with the outpouring of tongues or with water. It simply says "baptized."

I am inclined to believe this instance was water baptism. I say this without an extensive linguistics review. You see, on most other occasions, the writer of Acts was very specific about baptism in the Holy Spirit, especially when it led to speaking in tongues. However, in Acts 2:41, he does not say it was with the outpouring of tongues. Therefore, I believe water baptism came right after their confession of faith in this particular instance.

I further believe Acts 2:41 was referring to water baptism since water baptism marked the addition to the church. This would be the proper next step for these converts.

> Acts 2 [46]*And they, continuing daily with one accord in the temple, and breaking bread from house to house, did eat their meat with gladness and singleness of heart,* [47]*Praising God, and having favour with all the people. And the Lord added to the church daily such as should be saved.*

So what happened as a result of the Day of Pentecost were three of the greatest events in the history of Christianity. They were: 1) receiving salvation, which grants eternal life because of the work of Christ 2) water baptism to signify submission to the direction and authority of the church that Christ died for and 3) baptism in the Holy Spirit that grants the gift of tongues, empowering greatness as a witness for Christ.

The disciples and other believers were saved prior to the Pentecost outpouring. This happened by the grace of God through the indwelling presence of the Holy Spirit they received. This made them candidates to receive the baptism of the Holy Spirit at Pentecost. Speaking in tongues accompanied their genuine new experience. It was expressed publicly.

Chapter 12. What Tongues Does for Believers

Speaking in tongues lets you establish a new method of intimate communication with God at a level beyond what is otherwise possible. It fills the gaps between structured prayer and spiritual meditation.

peaking in tongues is clearly a gift from God that is reserved for born-again believers. Unfortunately, not all have experienced it. But this lack of experience makes it no less a wonderful gift. It allows the believer to know the unique, personal intimacy of God's presence. It is worth the spiritual effort to find your way to this gift and others. Paul encouraged the church to do so.

1 Corinthians 14 [1]...eagerly desire spiritual gifts...

Unfortunately, some within the body of Christ have difficulty understanding what speaking in tongues exactly does for them. To know what it does, you need only read 1 Corinthians 14. Speaking in tongues does exactly what these verses so plainly state.

1 Corinthians 14 [2]For anyone who speaks in a tongue does not speak to men but to God. Indeed, no one understands him; he utters mysteries with his spirit.

[4]He who speaks in a tongue edifies himself, but he who prophesies edifies the church.

One of the things speaking in tongues does is let you speak directly to God. This is done beyond the rudiments of your normal prayer life. It is truly a wonderful experience because it leaves you with no doubt about God's existence and desires for your life.

You get to know more about God's desires for you through your direct line to Him. This happens as a consequence of intimate contact. It is contact that is often difficult to get through learned prayer formats. But the Holy Spirit knows what you want and what your needs are. Speaking in tongues frees them to be verbally expressed without reservation.

Romans 8 ²⁶In the same way, the Spirit helps us in our weakness. We do not know what we ought to pray for, but the Spirit himself intercedes for us with groans that words cannot express.

You will also hear God speak back to you. You will know it is Him because His voice will be clear. His voice will provide great news directly to your spirit!

John 10 ²⁷My sheep listen to my voice; I know them, and they follow me. ²⁸I give them eternal life, and they shall never perish; no one can snatch them out of my hand.

You obviously do not have to speak in tongues to talk to God or hear Him talk back to you. Your learned prayer with meditation times work well for this. Verbal or silent prayer always has and always will get you in touch with God. Never doubt that it will.

Luke 18 ¹Then Jesus told his disciples a parable to show them that they should always pray and not give up.

You can also read what God wants you to know directly from the Bible. And since you are saved, the Holy Spirit will translate what you read into meaning for your life.

Hebrews 4 ¹²For the word of God is living and active. Sharper than any double-edged sword, it penetrates even to dividing soul and spirit, joints and marrow; it judges the thoughts and attitudes of the heart.

The written word of God, contained in the Bible, is the greatest and most secure way to obtain God's truth. So I am not suggesting you neglect Bible reading as a pathway to hearing from God. You must read God's word that is contained in the Bible! It is important to Christian growth, as it always has been.

Acts 17 ¹¹Now the Bereans [Christians] were of more noble character than the Thessalonians, for they received the message *with great eagerness and examined the Scriptures every day to see if what Paul said was true. [Revis annotation]*

God's word also lets you know that you can make spirit-to-spirit contact with God in a one-on-one fashion, through speaking in tongues. When you do, you discover a new personal level of communication intimacy, interacting with the same God that you already know from the Bible and through structured prayer.

Speaking in tongues lets you establish a new method of intimate communication with God at a level beyond what is otherwise possible. It fills the gaps between structured prayer and spiritual meditation.

Another thing speaking in tongues does is build up your spiritual nature. There is a component of your created nature that needs to be refueled directly from the spirit of God. Speaking in tongues lets this happen.

1 Corinthians 14 [4]He who speaks in a tongue edifies himself, but he who prophesies edifies the church.

God wants to leave a tangible event in your life to increase your spirit's stamina and aptitude. Speaking in tongues is one key way He does it. Speaking in tongues is a pathway to God by which the believer is refueled and strengthened in a miraculous way. With speaking in tongues, it does not take long for you to experience the impact of your new self!

Speaking in tongues is instant access to spiritual impartation that reenergizes the spirit-man to the best position before God.

Take a look again at Acts 10. In this event, the prophetic word brought about the tangible result of speaking in tongues, which comes by the baptism of the Holy Spirit.

> *Acts 10 ⁴⁴While Peter was still speaking these words, the Holy Spirit came on all who heard the message. ⁴⁵The circumcised believers [Christian Jews] who had come with Peter were astonished that the gift of the Holy Spirit had been poured out even on the Gentiles [non-Jewish converts]. ⁴⁶For they heard them speaking in tongues and praising God. [Revis annotation]*

As Peter was speaking, the baptism of the Holy Spirit came upon the gentiles. The reason they knew it was the baptism of the Holy Spirit was because the gentiles were speaking in tongues. The gentiles accepted the prophetic impartation from Peter and were baptized with the outpouring of tongues!

After Peter spoke, the gentile believers were endowed with speaking in tongues. The purpose of speaking in tongues was to build them up in a spiritual fashion that had not yet been achieved. Evidently, they were saved and gifted during the same event or within a relatively short time period.

It is worth mentioning that the Acts 10 account evidently was not the gift of a foreign language. There was no need for a foreign translation, since the people in this instance either spoke or understood a common language. They were hearing what Peter was saying very well before the outpouring of tongues was manifested. There was no communication gap for this group like there was on the Day of Pentecost. So there was no need for foreign language intervention. But there was a spiritual gap. There was a need to increase the power in these new converts. There was a need for edification or building up. Speaking in tongues was the unique spiritual way for this to happen.

Speaking in tongues builds you up in unique ways. For example, sometimes there is something in your spirit that needs to connect with the pure power of God's holiness. Your words might get in the way. Your words simply do not always let you make a genuine connection, despite your best spiritual efforts. When that happens, your true inner spirit can speak for you in tongues, by the Holy Spirit.

Romans 8 ²⁶In the same way, the Spirit helps us in our weakness. We do not know what we ought to pray for, but the Spirit himself intercedes for us with groans that words cannot express. ²⁷And he who searches our hearts knows the mind of the Spirit, because the Spirit intercedes for the saints in accordance with God's will.

With baptism of the Holy Spirit, your spirit will speak what is in your heart. It will pour out utterances that your personal speech habits did not design, learn or memorize. Your normal speech patterns and delivery will be overridden by an inward move of God's anointing. This will invite your innermost spiritual heart to speak out based on its overflow.

Luke 6 ⁴⁵The good man brings good things out of the good stored up in his heart, and the evil man brings evil things out of the evil stored up in his heart. For out of the overflow of his heart his mouth speaks.

So an important thing that speaking in tongues does for the believer is let him or her pour out what is contained in their heart-spirit. They pour out what is tucked away for a special time with God. The mouth then reflects what the spirit-man is saying without interference from the mental-man. When it happens, you might not personally understand it during the outpouring, but your spirit will. And you will experience the wonderful effect of it. You will know you have encountered a very special spiritually based moment in time with God.

1 Corinthians 14 ²For anyone who speaks in a tongue does not speak to men but to God. Indeed, no one understands him; he utters mysteries with his spirit. ³But everyone who prophesies

speaks to men for their strengthening, encouragement and comfort.
⁴He who speaks in a tongue edifies himself, but he who prophesies
edifies the church.

Speaking in tongues shortcuts getting difficult desires and hard-to-express needs over to God. He already knows about them. But speaking in tongues solicits a response by a purely spiritual communication channel. Speaking in tongues removes your personal, flesh-infested motives from being at the forefront of your conscience mind when you talk to God. In this way, whatever comes from your spirit is pure communication directly to God. Whatever the information, God gets it direct and without interference.

According to 1 Corinthians 14:2, speaking in tongues also lets you express or utter mysteries from the depths of your spirit. The exact identity of these mysteries is not altogether clear. But it is worth pointing out that the word "mysteries" in the Bible is often used to connote something of very special or extraordinary value; something precious.

The amplified version of the Bible says it well about God's mysteries. It calls them "secret truths." Again, the word secret tends to connote something special or of high value or very precious, yet not obvious to normal understanding and perception.

1 Corinthians 14 ²For one who speaks in an [unknown] tongue speaks not to men but to God, for no one understands or catches his meaning, because in the [Holy] Spirit he utters secret truths and hidden things [not obvious to the understanding]. (Amplified Bible)

Therefore, speaking in tongues lets the precious things of your life get through to God without being corrupted, contaminated or lost in translation.

So as unbelievable as speaking in tongues might sound, the episode is a true event. It happens in the life of a saved person. Speaking in tongues is very consistent with God's nature. It makes sense in the spiritual nature of God.

1 Corinthians 2 ¹⁴The man without the Spirit does not accept the things that come from the Spirit of God, for they are foolishness to him, and he cannot understand them, because they are spiritually discerned.

It is critical to your spiritual empowerment that certain key moves of God not get lost in translation. This is why the outpouring of tongues on the Day of Pentecost particularly resulted in a foreign language. This unique foreign language intervention allowed the word of God to reach potential converts of many nationalities and races without filtration through human interpretation. This transfer of the prophetic information was pure and unencumbered. It resulted in spirits becoming activated. Activation of the spirits led to saved lives!

That is how a spiritual move of God works. Something tangible results from what His spirit starts. In other words, you should see something visible resulting from a faith-filled encounter with God. Faith delivers what eyes cannot see, ears cannot hear, noses cannot smell and hands cannot touch.

Hebrews 11 ¹Now faith is the substance [tangible result] of things hoped for [spiritually conceived], the evidence of things not seen. ² For by it the elders obtained a good testimony.³ By faith we understand that the worlds were framed by the word of God, so that the things which are seen were not made of things which are visible. [Revis annotation]

The visible things we now have were started in the invisible spirit-heart of God. It was a spiritual conception that yielded a visible delivery to man.

So then, the finished work of God's spirit is a tangible result to man for his good. That good is especially deposited into the life of the believer. It is seen as tangible favor and blessings in the believer's life.

Psalm 1 ¹Blessed is the man who does not walk in the counsel of the wicked or stand in the way of sinners or sit in the seat of mockers. ²But his delight is in the law of the LORD, and on his law he meditates day and night. ³ He is like a tree planted by streams of water, which yields its fruit in season and whose leaf does not wither. Whatever he does prospers.

The outpouring of God's word at Pentecost was very precious. The mystery unfolded under the ordained power of the Holy Spirit by baptism with the evidence of speaking in tongues. So why would one dare say speaking in tongues is not an important gift to the church? Why would one think that God discontinued this blessing? To do so would be contrary to His nature.

One goal of speaking in tongues is to build you up while you are in the church. This is clearly stated by Paul. There is no ambiguity in this message.

1 Corinthians 14 ⁴He who speaks in a tongue edifies himself, but he who prophesies edifies the church.

Speaking in tongues builds you up individually just as prophecy collectively builds up the church body.

You do not want to be the weakest link when Satan attacks. You will need strength! The gift of tongues grants it to you.

1 Peter 5 ⁸Be self-controlled and alert [built up]. Your enemy the devil prowls around like a roaring lion looking for someone to devour. [Revis annotation]

God has no intention of letting you live a saved life under the feet of Satan. So God encoded your spirit with the ability to be built up before Satan is aware of it. That edification code is speaking in tongues. It puts your spirit in touch with God before the devil can get involved! Speaking in tongues locks the devil out of the communication loop between you and heaven.

With tongues, you are absolutely never without instant, pure access to God. And speaking in tongues does not violate the well-known avenues to God's presence. Speaking in tongues works in synergy with them. For example, Paul taught how speaking in tongues co-exists with prayer.

> *1 Corinthians 14* [14]*For if I pray in a tongue, my spirit prays, but my mind is unfruitful.* [15]*So what shall I do? I will pray with my spirit, but I will also pray with my mind; I will sing with my spirit, but I will also sing with my mind.* [16]*If you are praising God with your spirit, how can one who finds himself among those who do not understand say "Amen" to your thanksgiving, since he does not know what you are saying?* [17]*You may be giving thanks well enough, but the other man is not edified.*

1 Corinthians 14:14 clearly shows spiritual prayer as one significant benefit of speaking in tongues. This is a great benefit. It is often called "warfare" praying in some Christian circles.

However, praying in tongues should not necessarily be taken to only mean there is a problem or that you are under attack. You do not always need warfare prayer. Consequently, praying in tongues also allows your spirit to pray the prayer of thanksgiving, without being taught a particular language. This frees you to let what is inside unabatedly come out to God.

This form of praying without being taught demonstrates a very important spiritual principle. The principle is this:

Speaking in tongues lets you know that you do not always need clear words or perfect language to communicate with God.

This principle has even more impact when you consider that one of the obstacles the first disciples faced while following Jesus was their lack of knowledge about how to pray.

> *Luke 11 ¹One day Jesus was praying in a certain place. When he finished, one of his disciples said to him, "Lord, teach us to pray, just as John taught his disciples."*

Praying in tongues helps to remove the teaching barrier. Teaching often takes time, but gifting does not. Gifting is an instant deposit from God to work in a present situation, when allowed to freely operate. The spiritual outpouring of tongues circumvents the need to spend hours learning how to pray or how to organize your thoughts. The tongues language simply lets your spirit open up to God.

Prayer is a very serious and important spiritual event. You should never underestimate the power of proper prayer to God. But even at your most righteous, it is possible to fall short when trying to pray words. However, when your spirit is sincere, groans are sufficient to get God's attention!

Sometimes words are too self-serving to communicate your true intentions and proper needs to God. Jesus taught this lesson to his disciples about how simplicity and innocence works in prayer.

> *Luke 18 ¹⁰"Two men went up to the temple to pray, one a Pharisee and the other a tax collector. ¹¹The Pharisee stood up and prayed about himself: 'God, I thank you that I am not like other men— robbers, evildoers, adulterers—or even like this tax collector. ¹²I fast twice a week and give a tenth of all I get.' ¹³"But the tax collector stood at a distance. He would not even look up to heaven, but beat his breast and said, 'God, have mercy on me, a sinner.' ¹⁴"I tell you that this man, rather than the other, went home justified before God. For everyone who exalts himself will be humbled, and he who humbles himself will be exalted."*

Praying in tongues is a simple and innocent route to God's presence. It makes a spiritual plea for mercy directly to God on your behalf. Speaking in tongues also sends up pure praise. It does so without self-centered flattering words or confusion with regard to the intended message.

Praying in tongues is very humbling because you do not use any of your trained communication skills. The spirit is the communicator, not you. When you pray in tongues, you allow your spirit-heart to dominate the delivery of the message.

Speaking in tongues grants believers the ability and opportunity to interact with God at a level beyond human nature and beyond the reach of Satan. This ability comes by the baptism of the Holy Spirit.

> _1 Corinthians 14 [2]For one who speaks in an [unknown] tongue speaks not to men but to God, for no one understands or catches his meaning, because in the [Holy] Spirit he utters secret truths and hidden things [not obvious to the understanding]. (Amplified Bible)_

Chapter 13. Tongues at Pentecost

On the Day of Pentecost, the spiritual non-language of speaking in tongues was actually spoken and the Holy Spirit acted as the original interpreter for the listeners.

Christians of all denominations agree that the Acts 2 Day of Pentecost was one of the most significant days in the history of the Christian faith. It is heralded as the day believers clearly moved from the spiritual period of law to the period of grace. It is viewed as the true beginning of the New Testament period of God's working on earth.

On the Day of Pentecost, man received a clear manifestation of a move of God by the Holy Spirit. That move was accompanied by the gift of speaking in tongues. No one can deny the biblical fact that an event called speaking in tongues was introduced to mankind's culture on that day. It holds spiritual significance, even among the most conservative believers.

> *Acts 2 ¹When the day of Pentecost came, they were all together in one place. ²Suddenly a sound like the blowing of a violent wind came from heaven and filled the whole house where they were sitting. ³They saw what seemed to be tongues of fire that separated and came to rest on each of them. ⁴All of them were filled with the Holy Spirit and began to speak in other tongues as the Spirit enabled them.*

Most believers hold that speaking in tongues on the Day of Pentecost is best described as an event involving foreign languages. Most biblical scholars agree on this point as well.

> *Acts 2 ⁵Now there were staying in Jerusalem God-fearing Jews from every nation under heaven. ⁶When they heard this sound, a crowd came together in bewilderment, because each one heard them speaking in his own language. ⁷Utterly amazed, they asked: "Are not all these men who are speaking Galileans? ⁸Then how is it that each of us hears them in his own native language? ⁹Parthians, Medes and Elamites; residents of Mesopotamia, Judea and Cappadocia, Pontus and Asia, ¹⁰Phrygia and Pamphylia, Egypt and the parts of Libya near Cyrene; visitors from Rome ¹¹both Jews and converts to Judaism Cretans and Arabs—we hear them declaring the wonders of God in our own tongues!"*

As one moves further from Pentecost, speaking in tongues does not show itself as prominent as a foreign language. Instead, speaking in tongues tends to stand out more as spiritual utterances and non-language.

So there is some occasional debate over whether there is more than one form of spiritual tongues in the Bible. One form of spiritual tongues is said to be a foreign language, capable of language interpretation. Another form of spiritual tongues is said to be spirit-filled utterances, interpreted by spiritual intervention. The utterance form is often referred to as the heavenly or angelic language of tongues. Then there are some who would contend that speaking in tongues is nothing more than mere emotional outburst or mimicking of religious acts.

It might very well be true that there are at least two forms of spiritual tongues in the Bible. And there might certainly be times when emotionalism has resulted in mimicked noise, either by the less mature or the spiritually misinformed. But it is highly plausible that the true expression of tongues exists in only one form. This would mean that the Day of Pentecost outpouring was the same form as that occurring later in scripture.

I assure you that my position on this matter does not violate any of the well-established beliefs about this great event. Neither does it require any new theological thinking. It is simple a refined look at the question of whether speaking in tongues at Pentecost was significantly different from the other occurrences later in the Bible.

To grasp the revelation, you must first recall that the Day of Pentecost was a very, very important event. This was a great opportunity for the disciples to witness to a large audience about Jesus Christ. They had been told to remain there until they had received the necessary power. That power would come supernaturally from God by way of baptism of the Holy Spirit.

Acts 1 [8]But you will receive power when the Holy Spirit comes on you; and you will be my witnesses in Jerusalem, and in all Judea and Samaria, and to the ends of the earth.

The power would make them available for a very specific purpose. That purpose would be to convert non-believers to Christ. This would certainly work towards fulfilling the great commission left by Jesus.

Matthew 28 [18]Then Jesus came to them and said, "All authority in heaven and on earth has been given to me. [19]Therefore go and make disciples of all nations, baptizing them in the name of the Father and of the Son and of the Holy Spirit, [20]and teaching them to obey everything I have commanded you. And surely I am with you always, to the very end of the age."

The impact on the great commission alone made Pentecost one of the most important days in the history of mankind. Pentecost was the catalyst for the beginning of the New Testament church, a church dedicated to Jesus Christ as Lord and Savior through grace and not by law.

Acts 2 [46]Every day they continued to meet together in the temple courts. They broke bread in their homes and ate together with glad and sincere hearts, [47]praising God and enjoying the favor of all the people. And the Lord added to their number daily those who were being saved.

The Day of Pentecost was a great move of God towards salvation. Clearly no other event aside from the birth, death and resurrection of Christ could mean so much to the evangelism of the world. I do not think anyone would argue this point.

The impact of Pentecost is the key to what I will now offer about unified speaking in tongues in the Bible.

It is likely that each of the people who spoke in tongues at Pentecost actually spoke the non-language of spiritual utterances. However, as the listeners heard the sounds, the Holy Spirit transformed the utterances into the respective languages of those under a spirit of conviction. These converts later reported only that they heard their native language. They had no reason to report utterances at that time.

Thus, the apostles were actual speaking in the outpouring of utterances. Those utterance tongues were being directly interpreted to the listeners as their native language by the Holy Spirit, which is all they heard. This scenario would differ from the apostles actually saying the foreign language from their lips.

Let me say it again. The foreign language speaking means the apostles formed a foreign language in their heads under the Holy Spirit, which they then spoke. The utterance-speaking means the apostles spoke utterances that were interpreted by the Holy Spirit as foreign languages. This may be only a matter of semantics, but I am suggesting the latter. This means that tongues at Pentecost were identical to tongues elsewhere in the Bible.

It is reasonable to view the Bible as having only one form of tongues. And that form would originate as utterances. This is particularly evident when you read Acts 2:6-7 and then read Acts 2:12-13.

Acts 2 ⁶When they heard this sound, a crowd came together in bewilderment, because each one heard them speaking in his own language. ⁷Utterly amazed, they asked: "Are not all these men who are speaking Galileans?

Acts 2 ¹²Amazed and perplexed, they asked one another, "What does this mean? ¹³Some, however, made fun of them and said, "They have had too much wine."

If the apostles were speaking a foreign language, even the nonbelievers would have at least recognized that foreign words were being exchanged. But Acts 2:13 states that "some made fun of them." This means that not all the listeners comprehended that they were speaking foreign languages. This group went on to say, "They have had too much wine," instead of a reference to them speaking a foreign language. An outpouring originating as utterances explains both views of what people later reported about their experience at Pentecost.

So we find that Pentecost was a day of translated or interpreted utterances instead of words coming out of the apostles mouths initially as foreign languages.

> **In other words, on the Day of Pentecost, the spiritual non-language of tongues was actually spoken and the Holy Spirit acted as the original interpreter to the listeners.**

Furthermore, the act of the Holy Spirit to interpret the tongues is very consistent with Paul's instructions to have an interpreter present when speaking in tongues is occurring.

1 Corinthians 14 [27]If anyone speaks in a tongue, two – or at the most three – should speak, one at a time, and someone must interpret.

With regard to exactly who should be the interpreter, Paul does not give clear instructions. But Pentecost shows the Holy Spirit as the original interpreter. The Holy Spirit took the heavenly utterances and interpreted them directly into the foreign languages of those willing to believe the gospel.

There were God-fearing Jews at Pentecost. They needed salvation, not building up. Therefore, the Holy Spirit gave the interpretation of tongues as a prophetic call to repentance. This happened in the native languages of the regions represented there.

Acts 2 [5]Now there were staying in Jerusalem God-fearing Jews from every nation under heaven. [6]When they heard this sound, a crowd came together in bewilderment, because each one heard them speaking in his own language. [7]Utterly amazed, they asked: "Are not all these men who are speaking Galileans? [8]Then how is it that each of us hears them in his own native language? [9]Parthians, Medes and Elamites; residents of Mesopotamia, Judea and Cappadocia, Pontus and Asia, [10]Phrygia and Pamphylia, Egypt and the parts of Libya near Cyrene; visitors from Rome [11](both Jews and converts to Judaism Cretans and Arabs—we hear them declaring the wonders of God in our own tongues!" [12]Amazed and perplexed, they asked one another, "What does this mean?"

After this awesome outpouring of the Holy Spirit, Peter offered His inspired commentary on what Joel had already prophesied. This left no doubt that it was God at work and not a work of man.

Joel 2 [28]And afterward, I will pour out my Spirit on all people. Your sons and daughters will prophesy, your old men will dream dreams, your young men will see visions. [29]Even on my servants, both men and women, I will pour out my Spirit in those days.

It is certainly possible that God initially poured out the new gift of speaking in tongues as a foreign language at Pentecost and as spiritual utterances later. However, to pour out speaking in tongues solely as utterances that are spiritually interpreted is the most unified scenario. This means that speaking in tongues on the Day of Pentecost was the same as elsewhere in the Bible.

Chapter 14. Joel's Last Days and Pentecost

Whatever was happening at Pentecost was something Joel had prophesied, or at least was part of his prophecy.

The prophecy of Joel was preached by Peter on the Day of Pentecost. Peter was quite bold in his statements in correlating the events of Pentecost with Joel's prophecy.

There tend to be questions, good questions, about the place of Peter's commentary on Joel with regard to end-time prophecy and present-day events. One key question is whether the prophecy of Joel fully happens on the Day of Pentecost in Acts 2 or whether it is still to come at the final end-time.

There are some important facts in the scriptures themselves that can help you gain at least a refreshed view with regard to the place and value of Joel's prophecy.

Start by reading Joel 2:28-32, which are the verses of particular interest. As you read, remember that most prophecies had an immediate message for their time period and a pending message for a later period.

Joel 2 ²⁸"And afterward, I will pour out my Spirit on all people. Your sons and daughters will prophesy, your old men will dream dreams, your young men will see visions. ²⁹Even on my servants, both I will pour out my Spirit in those days. ³⁰I will show wonders in the heavens and on the earth, blood and fire and billows of smoke. ³¹The sun will be turned to darkness and the moon to blood before the coming of the great and dreadful day of the LORD. ³²And everyone who calls on the name of the LORD will be saved; for on Mount Zion and in Jerusalem there will be deliverance, as the LORD has said, among the survivors whom the LORD calls.

Many would like to interpret this prophecy solely as end-time. This would mean that your present time is excluded from it. And that would be correct to a large extent because this prophecy does involve a future end-time event as well. However, as you look at Peter's message, it becomes clear that a portion of Joel's prophecy was fulfilled at Pentecost, or at least began to be fulfilled.

One certainly must contemplate that the first portion of Peter's message, Acts 2:17-18 (Joel 2:28-29), was relevant to the time of Pentecost. It would then extend also to your present time. The later portion of the prophecy, Acts 2:19-20 (Joel 2:30-31), would be for the conclusive end-time day of the Lord. The time of that event is uncertain.

> *2 Peter 3 ¹⁰But the day of the Lord will come like a thief. The heavens will disappear with a roar; the elements will be destroyed by fire, and the earth and everything in it will be laid bare.*

Evidence of what time period Peter's preaching was referring to can be gained by letting other scripture interpret Acts 2:17-18. The preceding verse in Acts 2:16 is helpful towards this goal.

> *Acts 2 ¹⁴Then Peter stood up with the Eleven, raised his voice and addressed the crowd: "Fellow Jews and all of you who live in Jerusalem, let me explain this to you; listen carefully to what I say. ¹⁵These men are not drunk, as you suppose. It's only nine in the morning! ¹⁶No, this is what was spoken by the prophet Joel:*

Peter said this "is" what was spoken by the prophet Joel. So whatever was happening at Pentecost was something Joel had prophesied, or was at least part of his prophecy. He did not say "will be." He said "is," which is present tense. So why not just believe what the Bible simply says? It says in clear and simple terms, the word "is." This means Peter's present time!

There was an event happening on the Day of Pentecost that was foretold by the prophet Joel. Peter said "this" is what was spoken by the prophet Joel. The writings in Acts 2:12 and Act 2:16 can help with understanding what event "this" was referring to. Follow the word "this" as you read.

> *Acts 2 ¹² "Amazed and perplexed, they asked one another, What does this mean?"*

> *Acts 2 ¹⁶ "When they heard this sound, a crowd came together in bewilderment, because each one heard them speaking in his own language."*

The phrases "this mean" and "this sound" were referring to the noise that the crowd heard. The identity of the noise was speaking in tongues as utterances. This happened because of what commonly became known as baptism of the Holy Spirit.

> *Acts 2 ²Suddenly a sound like the blowing of a violent wind came from heaven and filled the whole house where they were sitting. ³They saw what seemed to be tongues of fire that separated and came to rest on each of them. ⁴All of them were filled with the Holy Spirit and began to speak in other tongues as the Spirit enabled them.*

The comment of the crowd about "sound" helps also deal with whether speaking in tongues at Pentecost was delivered verbally as spoken foreign languages. Had this been delivered solely as spoken foreign languages, it would have been recognized as such by the Jews in attendance. But some said they heard language and others reported hearing only noise or sounds. This suggests that utterances as tongues were spoken; and then the Holy Spirit interpreted the utterances into the ears of those with a heart to believe the spirit-inspired message.

> *Acts 2 ¹²Amazed and perplexed, they [those who heard their native language] asked one another, "What does this mean?" ¹³Some, however, made fun of them and said, "They have had too much wine." [Revis annotation]*

In either instance, on the Day of Pentecost, the crowd heard something called speaking in tongues. This happened on that very specific date in time in fulfillment of Joel 2:28-29.

With regard to the remaining portion of Joel 2:30-31, this is referring to the future end-time period of the tribulations as recorded in Revelation.

> *Revelation 6 ¹²I watched as he opened the sixth seal. There was a great earthquake. The sun turned black like sackcloth made of*

goat hair, the whole moon turned blood red, ¹³and the stars in the sky fell to earth, as late figs drop from a fig tree when shaken by a strong wind. ¹⁴The sky receded like a scroll, rolling up, and every mountain and island was removed from its place.

As a note, there is no requirement, when interpreting prophecy, that consecutive and sequential verses of scripture must refer to the same event. The Bible is not a pre-written novel with nice endings to fit your personal taste. So the fulfillment of Joel 2:28-29 at Pentecost does not mean that Joel 2:30-31 had to be fulfilled as well. The two sections stand alone.

Now we have looked at a portion of scripture to answer the question of whether Peter's message at Pentecost was referring to a present-time or end-time event. It showed that the Day of Pentecost outpouring was the fulfillment of a least a portion of Joel's prophecy. The fulfillment started what was called the "last days."

Acts 2 ¹⁷In the last days, God says, I will pour out my Spirit on all people. Your sons and daughters will prophesy, your young men will see visions, your old men will dream dreams.

Acts 2:17 says "days," which is plural; not "day," singular. Therefore, one would not look on this as a single, one-time event. Instead, this is best viewed as a period or season of God's working, with more to come.

We are currently in the last days or in the last season of God's grace upon mankind. How long to the final exact end-time of the Lord is uncertain. But clearly God initiated a new move upon the earth at Pentecost. I do not see evidence that it stopped then. It certainly was still active during Paul's ministry several years after Pentecost.

1 Corinthians 14 ¹⁸I thank God that I speak in tongues more than all of you.

Gifts are mechanisms by which the Holy Spirit manifests itself with us for authoritative power to win souls. Winning souls is for now. We cannot afford to wait until later!

> Acts 1 ⁸*But you will receive power when the Holy Spirit comes on you; and you will be my witnesses [now] in Jerusalem, and in all Judea and Samaria, and to the ends of the earth. [Revis annotation]*

We need Pentecostal experiences today! There is absolutely no reason to believe that we should not be walking under the same powerful anointing as the early church.

> Acts 2 ¹*When the day of Pentecost came, they were all together in one place. ²Suddenly a sound like the blowing of a violent wind came from heaven and filled the whole house where they were sitting. ³They saw what seemed to be tongues of fire that separated and came to rest on each of them. ⁴All of them were filled with the Holy Spirit and began to speak in other tongues as the Spirit enabled them.*

Speaking in tongues is a gift for the church now. Speaking in tongues testifies of the spiritual power of the church to operate in its earthly kingdom life for God while Christ is physically absent from man.

> John 14 ²⁶*But the Counselor, the Holy Spirit, whom the Father will send in my name, will teach you all things and will remind you of everything I have said to you.*

In the final end-time, we will return to a season of righteousness before Christ. We will not need the gifts at that time to operate within the church. Christ will solely and directly rule and administer eternally over us.

> Revelation 21 ²³*The city does not need the sun or the moon to shine on it, for the glory of God gives it light, and the Lamb [Jesus] is its lamp. [Revis annotation]*

So the last-days period mentioned in Acts 2:17 is the current time of grace leading up to the future end-time final rapture and tribulations events. The "last days" period started at Pentecost and is still active today.

Chapter 15. Why Words and Utterances

The utterance of sound in the form of words, speech, tongues, grunts and groans encourages faith back to the listener.

Whether the Acts 2 Day of Pentecost was an outpouring solely of a spiritual non-language form of tongues or an outpouring of the foreign languages might be debated by some. But what cannot be overlooked is that this was one of the most powerful outpouring of God's anointing of the Holy Spirit ever since the dawn of mankind! It was truly a miraculous baptism that resulted in unique sounds that had not been heard before in this manner. The sounds were clearly inspired by the Holy Spirit. They were gifted, not learned. The sounds were called speaking in tongues.

So the outcome of Pentecost in any regard was essentially the same. The Holy Spirit anointed people to speak in tongues!

Acts 2 ⁴All of them [in the room] were filled with the Holy Spirit and began to speak in other tongues as the Spirit enabled them. [Revis annotation]

Acts 2 ⁶When they [townspeople] heard this sound, a crowd came together in bewilderment, because each one heard them speaking in his own language. [Revis annotation]

But you might be wondering why speak at all? Why make a sound at all? Why make any utterances? In other words, could not the baptism of the Holy Spirit have left some sign other than verbal utterances?

Yes it could. The baptism of the Holy Spirit could have left a sign other than verbal tongues. But it did not! It chose to leave speaking in tongues. It chose to leave verbal evidence; a manifestation by way of verbal sound. So perhaps a better question is why sound at all?

To start with, the spiritual nature of God is such that sound works beyond just the noise component of the biological function. Speaking and hearing are designed to work together beyond the physical domain. Hearing what is spoken takes you into the spiritual domain of faith as well. Notice what the scripture says.

Romans 10 [17]Consequently, faith comes from hearing the message, and the message is heard through the word of Christ.

Hearing is a very important part of the faith walk and the faith cycle of life. The relationship of hearing to faith and the result thereof is emphasized quite frequently throughout the Bible.

Proverbs 18:21 Words can bring death or life! Talk too much, and you will eat everything you say.

The scripture is clear that we ought to consider what we say and what we hear very carefully. It also suggests very strongly that even pointless remarks that are spoken can have spiritual repercussions. Some might show up as negative, tangible consequences.

Proverbs 18 [21]The tongue has the power of life and death, and those who love it will eat its fruit.

Jesus used the power of speaking to bring Lazarus back from the death. He spoke to death and brought back life. Death heard the word of life and responded!

John 11:43 When he had said this, Jesus called in a loud voice, "Lazarus, come out!"

Notice that Jesus "called in a loud voice." In other words, Jesus made a very loud sound, as in a shout.

Why would Jesus do such a thing? Why would Jesus take time to speak loudly if sound had only a minor significance? Certainly Jesus could have brought Lazarus back by other means! So why did Jesus bother to utter noise? Just think about it for a moment; Jesus spoke loudly to a dead man to work a miracle. Why?

What you discover from this event is that sounds, noises, utterances and languages have a valued place within the faith process of God. There is faith-filled, spiritual value in what is spoken. It is particularly valuable when it is spoken under a prophetic anointing, or a voice of faith-filled authority.

Jesus spoke directly to Lazarus to bring him back to life. This demonstrates the principle of how faith-filled speaking invites the spirit to bring out new life.

> **Faith-filled speaking is an action of faith that causes a reaction from heaven that favors new life in you.**

Matthew 21 ²¹Jesus replied, "I tell you the truth, if you have faith and do not doubt, not only can you do what was done to the fig tree, but also you can say to [make sound to] this mountain, 'Go, throw yourself into the sea,' and it will be done. [Revis annotation]

Jesus spoke to Lazarus as a signal of one aspect of what the perfect will of God was originally intended to be with regard to communication. Sound was intended to be one mechanism for inviting a spiritual response. The spiritual response could be accompanied by a tangible outcome.

The teachings of Paul in Romans 10 support the contention that speaking and hearing sound carries spiritual significance.

Romans 10 ¹³for, "Everyone who calls on the name of the Lord will be saved." ¹⁴How, then, can they call on the one they have not believed in? And how can they believe in the one of whom they have not heard? And how can they hear without someone preaching to them?

Remember that God's actions start in the spirit realm and show up as tangible results. Speaking with utterances is part of His spiritual release process, whether or not we completely comprehend it.

God spoke to bring about the universe and our world as we know it. Throughout each step, the Bible records speaking as part of the creation process. In other words, God spoke to nothing and created something. He spoke to nowhere and created everywhere!

Genesis 1 ¹In the beginning God created the heavens and the earth. ²Now the earth was formless and empty, darkness was over the surface of the deep, and the Spirit of God was hovering over the waters. ³And God said, "Let there be light," and there was light.

Genesis 1 ⁶And God said, "Let there be an expanse between the waters to separate water from water."

Genesis 1 ⁹And God said, "Let the water under the sky be gathered to one place, and let dry ground appear." And it was so.

Genesis 1 ¹¹Then God said, "Let the land produce vegetation: seed-bearing plants and trees on the land that bear fruit with seed in it, according to their various kinds." And it was so.

Genesis 1 ¹⁴And God said, "Let there be lights in the expanse of the sky to separate the day from the night, and let them serve as signs to mark seasons and days and years, ¹⁵ and let them be lights in the expanse of the sky to give light on the earth." And it was so.

Genesis 1 ²⁰And God said, "Let the water teem with living creatures, and let birds fly above the earth across the expanse of the sky."

Genesis 1 ²⁴And God said, "Let the land produce living creatures according to their kinds: livestock, creatures that move along the ground, and wild animals, each according to its kind." And it was so.

After speaking the earth into being, including its structure and content, God spoke the creation of man into being. And why would God do such a thing when He, as the Trinity, was the only one there to hear it? It must have had specific spiritual value.

> *Genesis 1* *[26]Then God said, "Let us [The Trinity] make man in our image, in our likeness, and let them rule over the fish of the sea and the birds of the air, over the livestock, over all the earth, and over all the creatures that move along the ground." [Revis annotation]*

Uttering sound as speech, tongues, grunts or groans in someway encourages faith back to the listener. It also sends a faith action out to the situation. Although the exact language, dialect and expression may differ or be unclear, communicating by sound has value in the spiritual work of God.

The preferred will of God, or certainly the originally intended will of God, prior to the fall of man, was for speaking to be an intricate part of man's faith walk. God intended it to be a form by which He could interact on a personal basis with man.

The desire of God to interact by sound with man is also inferred by the conversation between Adam and God, even after Adam's fall from innocence.

> *Genesis 3* *[8]Then the man and his wife heard the sound of the LORD God as he was walking in the garden in the cool of the day, and they hid from the LORD God among the trees of the garden. [9]But the LORD God called to the man, "Where are you?" [10]He answered, "I heard you in the garden, and I was afraid because I was naked; so I hid."*

This was not a mental exchange between Adam and God. It was not telepathy. Neither was it an impression on Adam's heart. This was clear, verbal communication. God was speaking directly to Adam and Adam was speaking back to God with sound or utterances.

God created ears as part of Adam's physical anatomy. God used this feature to interact with Adam and instruct him. Adam likewise used hearing and speech to interact back with God. Essentially, what you have in this Genesis account is the original pattern by which God and man communicated. You have the spiritual God communicating with the physical man by speaking sounds that reaches man's ears. Man's ears are serving as collectors of information for his mind. They are also functioning as conduits to man's spirit.

God has always interacted with man by sounds. He speaks His will directly to men and women, especially those who have willing spirits to hear and then respond.

For example, God spoke to Noah to build the ark. God spoke by verbal sound to this physical man.

> *Genesis 6 [13]So God said to Noah, "I am going to put an end to all people, for the earth is filled with violence because of them. I am surely going to destroy both them and the earth. [14]So make yourself an ark of cypress wood; make rooms in it and coat it with pitch inside and out. [15]This is how you are to build it: The ark is to be 450 feet long, 75 feet wide and 45 feet high. [16]Make a roof for it and finish the ark to within 18 inches of the top. Put a door in the side of the ark and make lower, middle and upper decks. [17]I am going to bring floodwaters on the earth to destroy all life under the heavens, every creature that has the breath of life in it. Everything on earth will perish. [18]But I will establish my covenant with you, and you will enter the ark—you and your sons and your wife and your sons' wives with you. [19]You are to bring into the ark two of all living creatures, male and female, to keep them alive with you.*

This was not an impression upon Noah's heart or mind. The details were too exact. Noah heard an audible sound from God that had definable meaning. Noah responded in kind to God with sound and action.

So the original, perfect intent of God was for sound to be a part of the integration of God's spiritual will into the innermost spiritual nature of man. The converse was also true.

However, once sin entered the world, the consequences forced man to work outside of the preferred or perfect intent of God. Some of the consequences of perpetual sin on earth included health failures such as birth defects that caused hearing loss, among other physical ailments. Sin also weakened the spirit of man such that he was unable to properly speak back to God with harmonious clarity.

So the gift of tongues accomplishes two things. It produces the utterance of spiritually influenced sound that is directly interpretable by people for their benefit. And it puts people back on pure speaking terms with God.

The utterance of sound in the form of words, speech, tongues, grunts and groans encourages faith back to the listener.

So consider once again the events of Pentecost, when a unique sound was introduced to mankind. The form was that of utterances known as speaking in tongues.

Acts 2 ¹When the day of Pentecost came, they were all together in one place. ²Suddenly a sound like the blowing of a violent wind came from heaven and filled the whole house where they were sitting. ³They saw what seemed to be tongues of fire that separated and came to rest on each of them. ⁴All of them were filled with the Holy Spirit and began to speak in other tongues as the Spirit enabled them. ⁵Now there were staying in Jerusalem Godfearing Jews from every nation under heaven. ⁶When they heard this sound, a crowd came together in bewilderment, because each one heard them speaking in his own language.

The word "sound" was mentioned in Acts 2:2. In Acts 2:6, the people heard the "sound." It did not say the "feeling" of a blowing wind. It said the "sound" of a blowing wind. Although the people in the room did not know exactly what the sound was, they realized it was significant. They realized they were hearing a unique sound, unlike any they had encountered before.

So sound is a very important part of the faith actions of God. God uses sound for spiritual impartation to bring about change in the lives of people.

Revelation 2 ²⁹He who has an ear, let him hear what the Spirit says to the churches.

Speaking in tongues, with noises and utterances, is one of the faith-filled, sound actions that God placed in the church as a gift. It brings a new level of spiritual living to believers.

Chapter 16. Tongues and Physical Capabilities

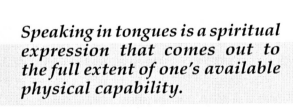

Speaking in tongues is a spiritual expression that comes out to the full extent of one's available physical capability.

God created ears and vocal cords in many of His creatures. They have very specific and practical physical functions for each species with regard to receiving and transmitting sound. Sound truly is a descriptive feature of nature as created by God.

In the case of man, God went beyond just the biological act. He created man with the ability to communicate by sound in both the physical and spiritual realm. In other words, God created the ears and voice of man to carry spiritual impact as well as physical. This act mirrors what the angels were originally created to do, which was to praise God eternally with sound.

> *Psalm 8 ⁴What is man, that thou art mindful of him? and the son of man, that thou visitest him? ⁵For thou hast made him a little lower than the angels, and hast crowned him with glory and honour.*

God expects us to use the full extent of the physical capabilities He created in us. This includes sound. For example, He encourages us to fully offer up sounds of praise and worship to Him as Lord.

> *Psalm 100 ¹Shout for joy to the LORD, all the earth. ²Worship the LORD with gladness; come before him with joyful songs.*

Speaking in tongues, with utterances, is one of audible sound acts of faith with which God gifted the church. It brings a new level of spiritual living to the church. The utterance of actual sound or noise is an important feature of this gift.

One of the reasons the utterance of sound or a verbal form is important when speaking in tongues can be understood by reading a portion of 1 Corinthian 14.

> *1 Corinthians 14 ²²Tongues, then, are a sign, not for believers but for unbelievers; prophecy, however, is for believers, not for unbelievers. ²³So if the whole church comes together and everyone*

speaks in tongues, and some who do not understand or some unbelievers come in, will they not say that you are out of your mind? ²⁴But if an unbeliever or someone who does not understand comes in while everybody is prophesying, he will be convinced by all that he is a sinner and will be judged by all, ²⁵and the secrets of his heart will be laid bare. So he will fall down and worship God, exclaiming, "God is really among you!"

In 1 Corinthians 14:22, it says the outward appearance of speaking in tongues is for the unbeliever. Speaking in tongues witnesses to unbelievers. The unbeliever receives an opportunity to observe the outpouring of God's anointing upon those who believe in Jesus Christ. And even though the unbeliever might reject it, the invitation to behold a manifestation of God is important, nonetheless. Audibly speaking in tongues extends this invitation.

Paul stresses, however, that witnessing to unbelievers by speaking in tongues should also have its appropriate boundaries and priority in expression. Out-of-order speaking in tongues or inopportune speaking in tongues could potentially hurt or become a distraction to the unbeliever.

1 Corinthians 14 ²³So if the whole church comes together and everyone speaks in tongues, and some who do not understand or some unbelievers come in, will they not say that you are out of your mind?

So then, speech and other utterances are important parts of the character of man's interactions with God. Utterances are also important aspects of witnessing to unbelievers. Sound and speech are creative forces of man. They have important spiritual value and impact.

The fall of man into sin disrupted the clarity and pure intent of speech, utterances and sound communication. The fallout of sin undeniably caused some of the physical malfunctions plaguing our world, including the lack of physical speech capabilities. Such losses are very saddening reminders of the reality of the consequences of sin. It affects even those who do not willfully commit sins.

John 9 ²His disciples asked him, "Rabbi, who sinned, this man or his parents, that he was born blind?" ³"Neither this man nor his parents sinned," said Jesus, "but this happened so that the work of God might be displayed in his life."

It is often difficult for us to admit, but sin's rule on earth can put severe limitation on our physical capabilities. The physical limitations often hamper the fullness of our spiritual expressions.

But physical ailments, including speech impairments, should not cause us to overlook God's originally ordained intent. That intent was for man to be spiritually and physically healthy, with audible speech.

3 John 1 ²Dear friend, I pray that you may enjoy good health and that all may go well with you, even as your soul is getting along well.

So faith-filled speaking in tongues establishes at least two clear things. One thing it establishes is unencumbered spiritual communication with God, according to His original intent in creation. This puts spiritual sounds back into the atmosphere that are consistent with God's desire. This is one way of combating Satan, who currently rules the earthly airways.

Ephesians 2 ¹As for you, you were dead in your transgressions and sins, ²in which you used to live when you followed the ways of this world and of the ruler of the kingdom of the air [KJV - prince of the power of the air], the spirit who is now at work in those who are disobedient. [Revis annotation]

A second thing that the verbal gift of speaking in tongues establishes is a credible witness to unbelievers that God is real and active in the lives of man. Such manifestations of

God by the Holy Spirit invite those listening to seek God's presence.

> *Acts 2 ³⁷Now when they heard this [tongues and prophecy], they were pricked in their heart, and said unto Peter and to the rest of the apostles, Men and brethren, what shall we do? ³⁸Then Peter said unto them, Repent, and be baptized every one of you in the name of Jesus Christ for the remission of sins, and ye shall receive the gift of the Holy Ghost. [Revis annotation]*

But what about people who cannot verbally speak for whatever physical reason? Can they also receive the gift of tongues? Of course they can! God does not hold a physical shortcoming against anyone. God accepts anyone and everyone who accepts him. He does it without discrimination with regard to physical, financial or social conditions. All one has to do is step up to the full extent of God's grace upon them.

> *Acts 10 ³⁴Then Peter began to speak: "I now realize how true it is that God does not show favoritism ³⁵but accepts men from every nation who fear him and do what is right.*

The gift of tongues is available to all saved believers in Jesus Christ; without regard to physical limitations. People who are saved, but can not verbally speak because of medically certifiable physical impairment, are not left out of God's gift of tongues. They can likewise be baptized by the Holy Spirit and receive the gift of tongues. A spiritual expression can rise up to God from within them, despite their physical condition.

The matter of capability is also one reason why the gift of tongues transcends being solely a foreign language. The gift of speaking in tongues as only a disguised foreign language limits the range of God's spiritual impartation. A foreign language limits speaking in tongues to only those who have the intellectual and physical capability to comprehend that particular language, even upon interpretation by the Holy

Spirit. This would particularly mean that people who cannot talk or hear would be omitted from this powerful gift.

But God's gifts are not confined to man's limitations and physical capabilities. They are well beyond them. So intellect, skill, speaking and hearing abilities do not limit the gifts of God.

Speaking in tongues is a spiritual expression that comes out to the full extent of one's available physical capability.

Therefore, those who either by birth or sickness or surgery cannot verbally speak are not left out. Those who cannot hear are not left out. They have the same access to God's spiritual gifts as other saved people. They have full access to the gifts of tongues. Their lack of audibly discernable expressions might limit their interaction with people for very practical and understandable reasons. But their approach to God is as open as those with verbally intelligible skills.

God expects all believers to live up to the full, physical extremes of His measure of grace upon them in all they do. This includes the spiritual aspects of life as well, like speaking in tongues.

Romans 12 ³For by the grace given me I say to every one of you: Do not think of yourself more highly than you ought, but rather think of yourself with sober judgment, in accordance with the measure of faith God has given you.

Ephesians 4 ⁷But to each one of us grace has been given as Christ apportioned it.

Chapter 17. The Conclusion of It All

Prophecy is the proclaimed word of God towards circumstances, and speaking in tongues is the manifested power of God at work in circumstances.

The gifts of prophecy and tongues are important to the development and growth of the church. Apostle Paul clarified the relationship between prophecy and speaking in tongues in 1 Corinthians 14. Paul taught that prophecy should have a priority within the church. However, he did not intend to imply that speaking in tongues should not be practiced at all by believers. On the contrary, Paul taught that speaking in tongues should be wisely used to build up believers in the church.

> *1 Corinthians 14 ¹Follow the way of love and eagerly desire spiritual gifts, especially the gift of prophecy. ²For anyone who speaks in a tongue does not speak to men but to God. Indeed, no one understands him; he utters mysteries with his spirit. ³But everyone who prophesies speaks to men for their strengthening, encouragement and comfort. ⁴He who speaks in a tongue edifies himself, but he who prophesies edifies the church. ⁵I would like every one of you to speak in tongues, but I would rather have you prophesy. He who prophesies is greater than one who speaks in tongues, unless he interprets, so that the church may be edified.*

There is generally good harmony among believers on the value and importance of prophecy. Unfortunately, speaking in tongues has stirred much debate, misrepresentation and religious bias. It has caused this gift to go lacking in many very good Christian assemblies. The debate has kept some faithful believers from experiencing the fullness of what God spiritually has for them and the church.

By examining God's word more closely, the purpose, priority and place of both prophecy and speaking in tongues can be better understood. Their places in the church can be seen more clearly.

In this book, I let the scripture speak for itself on the matter of spiritual gifts. Moreover, I let the scripture address the topic of speaking in tongues without traditional doctrine or denominational bias.

2 Timothy 2 *Do your best to present yourself to God as one approved, a workman who does not need to be ashamed and who correctly handles the word of truth.* *Avoid godless chatter, because those who indulge in it will become more and more ungodly.*

What you find by way of scripture is a wonderful synergy at work between the gifts of prophecy and tongues. But this is not surprising, since God is the author of both prophecy and tongues. And God does not work against Himself!

Mark 3 *If a house is divided against itself, that house cannot stand.*

1 Corinthians 14 *For God is not a God of disorder but of peace. As in all the congregations of the saints.*

God is at work in spiritual gifts. Therefore, it is difficult to imagine that any of the ordained Bible writers would set prophecy against speaking in tongues or speaking in tongues against prophecy. And they did not! The working of one makes the other more complete. Each gift must be respected for its individual contributions to the body of Christ.

Prophecy is the proclaimed word of God towards circumstances, and speaking in tongues is the manifested power of God at work in circumstances.

Prophecy and speaking in tongues work together to the glory of God. When prophecy is spoken, people are compelled to seek changed lives. When speaking in tongues pours out, the lives of those changed by prophecy are strengthened. Together, the gifts drive toward a more aligned and balanced relationship with God.

The first instance of the synergy between prophecy and speaking in tongues happened on the Day of Pentecost, after Jesus' ascension back to heaven. On that day, the Holy Spirit took up residence in the earth. The testimony of the Holy Spirit's presence was evidenced by speaking in tongues.

> Acts 2 [37]*When the people heard this [heard Peter preach, speak or prophesy], they were cut to the heart and said to Peter and the other apostles, "Brothers, what shall we do?" [38]Peter replied, "Repent and be baptized, every one of you, in the name of Jesus Christ for the forgiveness of your sins. And you will receive the gift of the Holy Spirit." [Revis annotation]*

Prophecy and speaking in tongues worked together to bring about the salvation of many on the Day of Pentecost. The synergy between the two gifts is undeniable. Anyone who is willing to forego religious dogma and preconceived biases will see it.

> 2 Corinthians 4 [3]*And even if our gospel [truth] is veiled, it is veiled to those who are perishing. [4]The god of this age has blinded the minds of unbelievers, so that they cannot see the light of the gospel of the glory of Christ, who is the image of God. [Revis annotation]*

When reading Paul's letter to the church at Corinth, it is difficult to conceive that he would be suggesting you not speak in tongues at all. And he was not. But rather, his letter was meant to only set the gift of tongues and the gift of prophecy in proper order. Paul said this very thing himself.

> 1 Corinthians 14 [5]*I would like every one of you to speak in tongues, but I would rather have you prophesy. He who prophesies is greater than one who speaks in tongues, unless he interprets, so that the church may be edified.*

> 1 Corinthians 14 [26]*What then shall we say, brothers? When you come together, everyone has a hymn, or a word of instruction, a revelation, a tongue or an interpretation. All of these must be done for the strengthening of the church.*

1 Corinthians 14 ³⁹So [to conclude], my brethren, earnestly desire and set your hearts on prophesying (on being inspired to preach and teach and to interpret God's will and purpose), and do not forbid or hinder speaking in [unknown] tongues. ⁴⁰But all things should be done with regard to decency and propriety and in an orderly fashion. (Amplified Bible)

Speaking in tongues results from baptism of the Holy Spirit. It occupies a valuable place in the spiritual development of the church. Speaking in tongues is the tangible outpouring of the Holy Spirit that is prophesied in God's word.

Luke 3 ¹⁶John answered, saying unto them all, I indeed baptize you with water; but one mightier than I cometh, the latchet of whose shoes I am not worthy to unloose: he shall baptize you with the Holy Ghost and with fire.

Acts 1 ⁸But you will receive power when the Holy Spirit comes on you; and you will be my witnesses in Jerusalem, and in all Judea and Samaria, and to the ends of the earth."

Mark 16 ¹⁷And these signs will accompany those who believe: In my name they will drive out demons; they will speak in new tongues.

The Day of Pentecost was the event that marked the new period of God's sovereign work with man to reveal His will. God used the gift of tongues to reveal His power on that day. He also used the gift of prophecy to communicate His purpose clearly to the crowd. The people heard both speaking in tongues and prophecy. They responded. Many were saved and themselves baptized in the Holy Spirit, with evidence of speaking in tongues.

The ultimate purpose of both prophecy and speaking in tongues is to give man an opportunity to repent and choose an eternal home with God. It is particularly awesome when they operate in tandem, yielding spiritual synergy.

2 Peter 3 ⁹The Lord is not slow in keeping his promise, as some understand slowness. He is patient with you, not wanting anyone to perish, but everyone to come to repentance.

Romans 10 ¹³for, "Everyone who calls on the name of the Lord will be saved." ¹⁴How, then, can they call on the one they have not believed in? And how can they believe in the one of whom they have not heard? And how can they hear without someone preaching to them?

Choosing Christ opens the door to one's eternal home with God. Using God's gifts wisely in the church helps believers live up to the full expectations God has for them. One of those expectations is to build towards spiritual maturity. Prophecy and speaking in tongues are two gifts that help.

Prophecy and speaking in tongues are expressions of spiritual inspiration. Prophecy comes forth when God inspires people to speak to the circumstances impacting man. Speaking in tongues occurs when the baptism of the Holy Spirit encourages a verbal outpouring to witness the presence of God with man. Both are important spiritual gifts that Paul encouraged the church to experience by properly prioritizing their respective operations.

1 Corinthians 14 ¹Follow the way of love and eagerly desire spiritual gifts, especially the gift of prophecy.

1 Corinthians 14 ³⁹Therefore, my brothers, be eager to prophesy, and do not forbid speaking in tongues.

1 Corinthians 14 ⁴⁰But everything should be done in a fitting and orderly way.

Paul did not set prophecy and speaking in tongues against each other in 1 Corinthian 14. The work of God was too important to do such a thing. Instead, Paul encouraged the church to keep God's gifts in order so as to benefit the church and all of mankind.

There really is no need for debates on the subject of prophecy or speaking in tongues. Salvation is too important to squander time on such frivolous undertakings. Prophecy is a gift from God. Speaking in tongues is also a gift from God.

> *1 Corinthians 14* [4]*He who speaks in a tongue edifies himself, but he who prophesies edifies the church.*

Chapter 18. The Clarity of Scripture

The word of God is the only way to truly silence the debate on speaking in tongues, once and for all. It is the best way to overcome the biases created by religious philosophies and social opinions.

There has been considerable debate on the topic of speaking in tongues and its place in today's church. It is a debate that is long overdue for a rest.

Some would hold that speaking in tongues is not a gift for today's church. Their position would be that the gift of tongues is an antiquated relic from the Day of Pentecost that ceased shortly after it began. Then others might say that speaking in tongues is not a gift at all. They would rather believe that the Day of Pentecost was an isolated incident that was sent only to introduce the New Testament church to the presence of the Holy Spirit. And yet others might even say that speaking in tongues is a gift, but it has limited relevance in the modern, sophisticated church. It would be their position that this is such a spiritualized, emotional encounter that would be best left to religious fanatics, church extremists and the uneducated.

But there need not be a debate. We have the word of God to settle the issue. The word of God is the only way to truly silence the debate on speaking in tongues, once and for all. It is the best way to overcome the biases created by religious philosophies and social opinions.

Hebrews 4 [12] For the word of God is living and active. Sharper than any double-edged sword, it penetrates even to dividing soul and spirit, joints and marrow; it judges the thoughts and attitudes of the heart.

The remainder of this chapter will give you the opportunity to read God's word on the topic of speaking in tongues for yourself. It will do so without interruption by commentary. It will include the entire chapter of 1 Corinthians 14 at the end.

Now let the word of the Lord speak clearly to you, by the power of the Holy Spirit. This is your personal wake-up call!

Prophetic Promise of Baptism of the Holy Spirit

Luke 3 ¹⁶John answered, saying unto them all, I indeed baptize you with water; but one mightier than I cometh, the latchet of whose shoes I am not worthy to unloose: he shall baptize you with the Holy Ghost and with fire.

John 14 ²⁶But the Counselor, the Holy Spirit, whom the Father will send in my name, will teach you all things and will remind you of everything I have said to you.

Mark 16 ¹⁷And these signs will accompany those who believe: In my name they will drive out demons; they will speak in new tongues;

Acts 1 ⁴On one occasion, while he was eating with them, he gave them this command: "Do not leave Jerusalem, but wait for the gift my Father promised, which you have heard me speak about. ⁵For John baptized with water, but in a few days you will be baptized with the Holy Spirit."

Acts 1 ⁸But you will receive power when the Holy Spirit comes on you; and you will be my witnesses in Jerusalem, and in all Judea and Samaria, and to the ends of the earth."

Pentecostal Fulfillment of Tongues

Acts 2 ¹When the day of Pentecost came, they were all together in one place. ²Suddenly a sound like the blowing of a violent wind came from heaven and filled the whole house where they were sitting. ³They saw what seemed to be tongues of fire that separated and came to rest on each of them. ⁴All of them were filled with the Holy Spirit and began to speak in other tongues as the Spirit enabled them.

Prophetic Impartation after Tongues

Acts 2 [14]Then Peter stood up with the Eleven, raised his voice and addressed the crowd: "Fellow Jews and all of you who live in Jerusalem, let me explain this to you; listen carefully to what I say. [15]These men are not drunk, as you suppose. It's only nine in the morning! [16]No, this is what was spoken by the prophet Joel: [17]"'In the last days, God says, I will pour out my Spirit on all people. Your sons and daughters will prophesy, your young men will see visions, your old men will dream dreams. [18]Even on my servants, both men and women, I will pour out my Spirit in those days, and they will prophesy.

Changed Lives and Perpetual Gifting Promised

Acts 2 [37]When the people heard this, they were cut to the heart and said to Peter and the other apostles, "Brothers, what shall we do?" [38]Peter replied, "Repent and be baptized, every one of you, in the name of Jesus Christ for the forgiveness of your sins. And you will receive the gift of the Holy Spirit. [39]The promise is for you and your children and for all who are far off—for all whom the Lord our God will call."

The Gift of Tongues Spreads

Acts 8 [14]When the apostles in Jerusalem heard that Samaria had accepted the word of God, they sent Peter and John to them. [15]When they arrived, they prayed for them that they might receive the Holy Spirit, [16]because the Holy Spirit had not yet come upon any of them; they had simply been baptized into the name of the Lord Jesus. [17]Then Peter and John placed their hands on them, and they received the Holy Spirit.

Acts 10 [44]While Peter was still speaking these words, the Holy Spirit came on all who heard the message. [45]The circumcised believers who had come with Peter were astonished that the gift of the Holy Spirit had been poured out even on the Gentiles. [46]For they heard them speaking in tongues and praising God.

Acts 19 ¹While Apollos was at Corinth, Paul took the road through the interior and arrived at Ephesus. There he found some disciples ²and asked them, "Did you receive the Holy Spirit when you believed?" They answered, "No, we have not even heard that there is a Holy Spirit." ³So Paul asked, "Then what baptism did you receive?" "John's baptism," they replied. ⁴Paul said, "John's baptism was a baptism of repentance. He told the people to believe in the one coming after him, that is, in Jesus." ⁵On hearing this, they were baptized into the name of the Lord Jesus. ⁶When Paul placed his hands on them, the Holy Spirit came on them, and they spoke in tongues and prophesied.

Gifts to the Church Includes Tongues

1 Corinthians 12 ⁸To one there is given through the Spirit the message of wisdom, to another the message of knowledge by means of the same Spirit, ⁹to another faith by the same Spirit, to another gifts of healing by that one Spirit, ¹⁰to another miraculous powers, to another prophecy, to another distinguishing between spirits, to another speaking in different kinds of tongues, and to still another the interpretation of tongues.

Gifts Prioritized by Love

1 Corinthians 13 ¹If I speak in the tongues of men and of angels, but have not love, I am only a resounding gong or a clanging cymbal.

1 Corinthians 13 ⁸Love never fails. But where there are prophecies, they will cease; where there are tongues, they will be stilled; where there is knowledge, it will pass away.

Prophecy and Tongues in the Church Clarified

1 Corinthians 14 ¹Follow the way of love and eagerly desire spiritual gifts, especially the gift of prophecy. ²For anyone who speaks in a tongue does not speak to men but to God. Indeed, no one understands him; he utters mysteries with his spirit. [3]But everyone who prophesies speaks to men for their strengthening, encouragement and comfort. [4]He who speaks in a tongue edifies himself, but he who prophesies edifies the church. [5]I would like every one of you to speak in tongues, but I would rather have you prophesy. He who prophesies is greater than one who speaks in tongues, unless he interprets, so that the church may be edified.

1 Corinthians 14 [6]Now, brothers, if I come to you and speak in tongues, what good will I be to you, unless I bring you some revelation or knowledge or prophecy or word of instruction? [7]Even in the case of lifeless things that make sounds, such as the flute or harp, how will anyone know what tune is being played unless there is a distinction in the notes? [8]Again, if the trumpet does not sound a clear call, who will get ready for battle? [9]So it is with you. Unless you speak intelligible words with your tongue, how will anyone know what you are saying? You will just be speaking into the air. [10]Undoubtedly there are all sorts of languages in the world, yet none of them is without meaning. [11]If then I do not grasp the meaning of what someone is saying, I am a foreigner to the speaker, and he is a foreigner to me. [12]So it is with you. Since you are eager to have spiritual gifts, try to excel in gifts that build up the church.

1 Corinthians 14 [13]For this reason anyone who speaks in a tongue should pray that he may interpret what he says. [14]For if I pray in a tongue, my spirit prays, but my mind is unfruitful. [15]So what shall I do? I will pray with my spirit, but I will also pray with my mind; I will sing with my spirit, but I will also sing with my mind. [16]If you are praising God with your spirit, how can one who finds himself among those who do not understand say "Amen" to your thanksgiving, since he does not know what you are saying? [17]You may be giving thanks well enough, but the other man is not edified.

1 Corinthians 14 [18]I thank God that I speak in tongues more than all of you. [19]But in the church I would rather speak five intelligible words to instruct others than ten thousand words in a tongue.

1 Corinthians 14 [20]*Brothers, stop thinking like children. In regard to evil be infants, but in your thinking be adults.* [21]*In the Law it is written: "Through men of strange tongues and through the lips of foreigners I will speak to this people, but even then they will not listen to me," says the Lord.*

1 Corinthians 14 [22]*Tongues, then, are a sign, not for believers but for unbelievers; prophecy, however, is for believers, not for unbelievers.* [23]*So if the whole church comes together and everyone speaks in tongues, and some who do not understand or some unbelievers come in, will they not say that you are out of your mind?* [24]*But if an unbeliever or someone who does not understand comes in while everybody is prophesying, he will be convinced by all that he is a sinner and will be judged by all,* [25]*and the secrets of his heart will be laid bare. So he will fall down and worship God, exclaiming, "God is really among you!"*

1 Corinthians 14 [26]*What then shall we say, brothers? When you come together, everyone has a hymn, or a word of instruction, a revelation, a tongue or an interpretation. All of these must be done for the strengthening of the church.* [27]*If anyone speaks in a tongue, two—or at the most three—should speak, one at a time, and someone must interpret.* [28]*If there is no interpreter, the speaker should keep quiet in the church and speak to himself and God.*

1 Corinthians 14 [29]*Two or three prophets should speak, and the others should weigh carefully what is said.* [30]*And if a revelation comes to someone who is sitting down, the first speaker should stop.* [31]*For you can all prophesy in turn so that everyone may be instructed and encouraged.* [32]*The spirits of prophets are subject to the control of prophets.* [33]*For God is not a God of disorder but of peace. As in all the congregations of the saints,* [34]*women should remain silent in the churches. They are not allowed to speak, but must be in submission, as the Law says.* [35]*If they want to inquire about something, they should ask their own husbands at home; for it is disgraceful for a woman to speak in the church.*

1 Corinthians 14 [36]*Did the word of God originate with you? Or are you the only people it has reached?* [37]*If anybody thinks he is a prophet or spiritually gifted, let him acknowledge that what I am writing to you is the Lord's command. ³⁸If he ignores this, he himself will be ignored.*

1 Corinthians 14 ³⁹Therefore, my brothers, be eager to prophesy, and do not forbid speaking in tongues. ⁴⁰But everything should be done in a fitting and orderly way.

You have now read God's word for yourself about the gift of tongues. I am sure it was a wonderful experience! You see the clarity that scripture brings to the topic of speaking in tongues. You now know that speaking in tongues is not as complicated as it might have once seemed. Thank God for the revelation!

The shackles have been broken from your mind about the gift of tongues. It is a gift for you! Now prepare to hear God speak to you in a fresh new way. And prepare to speak back to Him like you never have before. When you do, God will begin to reveal more insights to you about speaking in tongues and how it is to personally impact your life. You will begin to speak back to Him in a fresh, new language about the changes your spirit-heart is experiencing.

The Holy Spirit is about to change your life. Let it do so by baptism of the Holy Spirit, with the evidence of speaking in tongues!

Chapter 19. God's Desire for You

The gift of speaking in tongues is your tangible, verbal expression of faith that testifies that the baptism of the Holy Spirit has raised and empowered your spiritual aptitude.

The ultimate desire of God is for you to go to heaven. This is His desire for all people. He sent Jesus Christ to secure everyone the right to repent and be saved, thereby gaining access to eternal life in heaven.

2 Peter 3 ⁹The Lord is not slow in keeping his promise, as some understand slowness. He is patient with you, not wanting anyone to perish, but everyone to come to repentance.

John 3 ¹⁶"For God so loved the world that he gave his one and only Son, that whoever believes in him shall not perish but have eternal life. ¹⁷For God did not send his Son into the world to condemn the world, but to save the world through him.

Romans 10 ¹³For whosoever shall call upon the name of the Lord shall be saved.

Hopefully, you have already made the decision to receive Jesus Christ. If you have, then you are saved. Now God wants you to help others find Jesus. He wants you to be an instrument for helping someone else experience the redeeming power of the gospel.

Matthew 28 ¹⁸Then Jesus came to them and said, "All authority in heaven and on earth has been given to me. ¹⁹Therefore go and make disciples of all nations, baptizing them in the name of the Father and of the Son and of the Holy Spirit, ²⁰and teaching them to obey everything I have commanded you. And surely I am with you always, to the very end of the age."

Ephesians 6 ¹⁹Pray also for me, that whenever I open my mouth, words may be given me so that I will fearlessly make known the mystery of the gospel, ²⁰for which I am an ambassador in chains. Pray that I may declare it fearlessly, as I should.

Being saved adds people to the church. That is how you got there. You were saved into the church by the divine, grace-filled action of the Holy Spirit.

The church is the family of God. It is the place of God's family structure and family order. It is God's incubator for spiritual growth as a member of the family. There is no better spiritual place to be than in the church.

The church has Jesus Christ as its authorized head. This gives the church personal credibility and power directly from heaven.

Ephesians 1 [18]I pray also that the eyes of your heart may be enlightened in order that you may know the hope to which he has called you, the riches of his glorious inheritance in the saints, [19]and his incomparably great power for us who believe. That power is like the working of his mighty strength, [20]which he exerted in Christ when he raised him from the dead and seated him at his right hand in the heavenly realms, [21]far above all rule and authority, power and dominion, and every title that can be given, not only in the present age but also in the one to come. [22]And God placed all things under his feet and appointed him to be head over everything for the church, [23]which is his body, the fullness of him who fills everything in every way.

Christ is also the one who makes the church a place of hope. It is hope for now and for the future. The church is a secure place for you to spiritually live because it will never be defeated!

Matthew 16 [18]And I tell you that you are Peter, and on this rock I will build my church, and the gates of Hades will not overcome it.

God really loves His church. And God wants His church to grow in a direction that brings people closer to Him. Therefore, He sends gifts to the church to orchestrate His desire for a wholesome and healthy, earthly home. He wants you to live a full, meaningful life as part of His church family.

God also sends gifts to aid your connection back to Him in a tangible, intimate way. His gifts let you get to know Him without the biases of the natural tendencies of human behavior. Even when those tendencies seem so right, they can actually be so wrong.

> *Proverbs 14* [12] *There is a way that seems right to a man, but in the end it leads to death.*

God's gifts to the church are deposited by the Holy Spirit. They have very specific purposes. These gifts are often guided by pastoral officials within the local church assembly. The pastoral officials nourish the growth and expansion of God's gifts for the benefit of all.

> *1 Corinthians 12* [28] *And in the church God has appointed first of all apostles, second prophets, third teachers, then workers of miracles, also those having gifts of healing, those able to help others, those with gifts of administration, and those speaking in different kinds of tongues.*

Apostle Paul filled a major pastoral role for much of the early church. He wrote 1 Corinthians 14 to put order back in the church with regard to the works of prophecy and speaking in tongues. He did not set these two gifts against each other.

> *1 Corinthians 14* [5] *I would like every one of you to speak in tongues, but I would rather have you prophesy. He who prophesies is greater than one who speaks in tongues, unless he interprets, so that the church may be edified.*

Do not neglect prophecy. Do not neglect speaking in tongues. These gifts are precious spiritual endowments from heaven. Prophecy will guide you into salvation. It will also direct your path as you live a saved life. Speaking in tongues will strengthen your spiritual demeanor, character and ability to witness more effectively as a saved person. Speaking in tongues will also reconfirm your relationship with God by putting you on spiritual speaking terms directly with Him.

> *1 Corinthians 14 ²For anyone who speaks in a tongue does not speak to men but to God. Indeed, no one understands him; he utters mysteries with his spirit.*

If you are saved, then prophecy has already impacted your life. You have experienced one of the most wonderful blessings ever. You are saved because of the indwelling power of the Holy Spirit within you. There is no turning back now. Your future is secure!

> *John 10 ²⁸I give them eternal life, and they shall never perish; no one can snatch them out of my hand.*

> *Romans 8 ¹So now there is no condemnation for those who belong to Christ Jesus.*

You live for Christ! Salvation by grace made it possible. Therefore, you have been set free from having to conform to religious expectation. That yoke has been broken from your life.

> *Galatians 5 ¹It is for freedom that Christ has set us free. Stand firm, then, and do not let yourselves be burdened again by a yoke of slavery.*

Speaking in tongues can have a similar impact in your life as that of prophecy. It is not the same as prophecy. But it does not have to be. The gift of tongues stands on its own spiritual merit. It has its own value to you in the body of Christ. There is no good reason to debate its validity or power. There is no reason to be ashamed of its method of expression. It is operating in accordance with the divine specifications and nature of God. It is part of how gospel living is expressed. So do not be ashamed of it, even as you are not ashamed of the prophetic word of the gospel and its power.

> *Romans 1 ¹⁶I am not ashamed of the gospel, because it is the power of God for the salvation of everyone who believes: first for the Jew, then for the Gentile.*

Like prophecy, speaking in tongues is a present-day, active gift. It is clearly supported by God's prophetic word as recorded in the Bible. Because speaking in tongues came by way of prophecy, it must return an eternal reward to you. Speaking in tongues will work in your life to bring fresh, spiritual results. It will raise your spiritual aptitude. Expect it!

> *Ecclesiastes 11 ¹Cast your bread upon the waters, for after many days you will find it again.*

> *Isaiah 55 ¹¹so is my word that goes out from my mouth: It will not return to me empty, but will accomplish what I desire and achieve the purpose for which I sent it.*

The gift of speaking in tongues has a unique place and specific priority within the church. It should not be denied its place and purpose in your life.

The gift of tongues is your tangible, verbal expression of faith that testifies that the baptism of the Holy Spirit has raised and empowered your spiritual aptitude.

Has it happened to you yet? Has the gift of tongues risen to the level of a verbal expression in your life? Has the gift of tongues risen from within your spirit and exited your mouth? If it has, be thankful for the experience of its awesome power.

But if you are saved and have not verbally expressed tongues from your mouth, now is the time to do it. It is time for speaking in tongues to come alive in you!

The gift of tongues will leave you with a refreshing, spirit-filled verbal encounter unlike any you have ever experienced. It might even want to do so at the most inopportune times and in the most unlikely places. Its driving power is undeniable.

So this is your opportunity to speak in tongues. Ready or not, here it comes! Receive the baptism of the Holy Spirit right where you are. Now let the Holy Spirit bring its verbal expression from your mouth today. Give God the praise!

Psalm 51 [15]O Lord, open my lips, and my mouth will declare your praise.

Eagerly desire spiritual gifts!

About the Author

D R. Anthony Revis is the founder and pastor of Faith Ministries Church, located in Midland, Michigan. His ministry style and prophetic look at God's word is refreshing and appealing to believers of all ages. He is author of *ROCK Your Relationships*, published by Authorhouse. He is also author of *Praise the Power that Refreshes* and *Your Image*, both self-published by Anthony Revis Ministries. He is also founder of ARM Bible Training Institute, located in Midland, Michigan.

Printed in the United States
48573LVS00002B/139-186

9 781425 920524